More Praise for *Pharmacy on a Bicycle*

"So many of the solutions to the world's most tragic health-care problems are simple and inexpensive—if we can get them to the people who need them most. Bing and Epstein show how that can be done by unleashing the entrepreneurial spirit of the world's poor."

—Sir Fazle Hasan Abed, KCMG, founder and Chairperson, BRAC

"Bing and Epstein show how people from around the world are creating successful innovative, 'outside the box' solutions to take health services the last mile. Stakeholders across the public, private, and nonprofit sectors will find the lessons shared in this book highly useful."

—Dr. Agnes Binagwaho, Minister of Health, Republic of Rwanda

"Bing and Epstein tackle the most important problem vexing global development: how do we spread what we know works to places and people who need it? This book offers powerful frameworks and examples that spark practical insights into what it will take to truly solve many of our most challenging problems."

—Jeff Bradach, cofounder and Managing Partner, The Bridgespan Group

"Drs. Bing and Epstein remind us that many of the deaths and much of the disease among mothers and children can be halted through simple and low-cost solutions. They combine their medical knowledge with cutting-edge business school methodologies to identify and summarize the opportunity for innovative solutions to combat disease and poverty. It's a must-read for people who care deeply about the world's poorest people."

—Peter Hotez, MD, PhD, Dean, National School of Tropical Medicine, Baylor
College of Medicine, and President, Sabin Vaccine Institute

"If you ever wondered why easily preventable and curable diseases cripple human potential across the developing world, this book has answers. Bing and Epstein are on a mission to make sure that access to basic health care is never a barrier for anyone to reach his or her full potential. This book will leave you with the hope that seemingly insurmountable development challenges can be transformed into solvable problems when creative partnerships are formed across sectors and mutual accountability is established."

—Ambassador Sally Cowal, Senior Vice President and Chief Liaison Officer, PSI

"*Pharmacy on a Bicycle* is about saving lives—simply, effectively, and inexpensively. Through their focus on innovative and entrepreneurial solutions, Bing and Epstein show how to take health care the last mile—to a place that's accessible, in a way that's acceptable, and at a cost that's affordable. Chock full of successful examples of ways this is already happening, it will leave you inspired and filled with hope!"

—Rich Stearns, President, World Vision USA

"While so much of the focus on health is a debate about the science, *Pharmacy on a Bicycle* is a timely reminder that simple, cost-effective solutions exist and can be scaled to provide access to quality care. A practical guide to successful program delivery—showing how millions of lives can be saved globally."
—Paul Bernstein, CEO, Pershing Square Foundation

"Bing and Epstein have clearly and powerfully described the global health challenge of the coming decade. The treatments to save millions of lives already exist, but governments, companies, and NGOs must embrace a new paradigm to convert medical discoveries into real-world solutions. Bing and Epstein's elegant framework for action provides clear guidance and a multitude of compelling examples to demonstrate that the power to save lives is already in our hands."
—Mark Kramer, Senior Fellow, Harvard University, and founder and Managing Director, FSG

"This is the first book I know of that goes beyond inspiring stories of social entrepreneurs to provide a comprehensive and practical guide to the entrepreneurial process itself. Every policy maker and aspiring social entrepreneur will benefit from the practical steps to successful entrepreneurship articulated in this book."
—Kirk O. Hanson, University Professor and Executive Director, Markkula Center for Applied Ethics, Santa Clara University

"We firmly believe that the world can dissociate health care from affluence. Change in policies is all we need to turn this dream into reality. *Pharmacy on a Bicycle* has many valuable propositions to make it happen."
—Dr. Devi Shetty, Chairman, Narayana Hrudayalaya Group of Hospitals, Bangalore, India

"Bing and Epstein have written an extremely readable and absorbing book that will be essential for any organization interested in empowering underserved populations to improve their health and well-being. Bravo!"
—Stanley S. Litow, Vice President of Corporate Citizenship and Corporate Affairs, IBM, and President, IBM International Foundation

Pharmacy on a Bicycle

Pharmacy on a Bicycle

Innovative Solutions for Global Health and Poverty

ERIC G. BING

and

MARC J. EPSTEIN

BK

Berrett–Koehler Publishers, Inc.
San Francisco
a BK Currents book

Copyright © 2013 by Eric G. Bing and Marc J. Epstein

Berrett-Koehler Publishers, Inc.
235 Montgomery Street, Suite 650
San Francisco, CA 94104-2916
Tel: (415) 288-0260   Fax: (415) 362-2512
www.bkconnection.com

Ordering Information

Quantity sales. Special discounts are available on quantity purchases by corporations, associations, and others. For details, contact the "Special Sales Department" at the Berrett-Koehler address above.
Individual sales. Berrett-Koehler publications are available through most bookstores. They can also be ordered directly from Berrett-Koehler: Tel: (800) 929-2929; Fax: (802) 864-7626; www.bkconnection.com.
Orders for college textbook/course adoption use. Please contact Berrett-Koehler: Tel: (800) 929-2929; Fax: (802) 864-7626.
Orders by U.S. trade bookstores and wholesalers. Please contact Ingram Publisher Services, Tel: (800) 509-4887; Fax: (800) 838-1149; E-mail: customer.service@ingram publisherservices.com; or visit www.ingrampublisherservices.com/Ordering for details about electronic ordering.

Berrett-Koehler and the BK logo are registered trademarks of
Berrett-Koehler Publishers, Inc.

Printed in the United States of America

Berrett-Koehler books are printed on long-lasting acid-free paper. When it is available, we choose paper that has been manufactured by environmentally responsible processes. These may include using trees grown in sustainable forests, incorporating recycled paper, minimizing chlorine in bleaching, or recycling the energy produced at the paper mill.

Library of Congress Cataloging-in-Publication Data

Bing, Eric G.
Pharmacy on a bicycle : innovative solutions to global health and poverty / Eric G. Bing and Marc J. Epstein.
     pages cm
ISBN 978-1-60994-789-7 (hardback)
1. Pharmaceutical policy--Developing countries. 2. Drugs--Developing countries. 3. Medical care--Developing countries. 4. World health. I. Epstein, Marc J. II. Title.
RA401.D44B53 2013
362.17'82091724--dc23   2013001871

First Edition
18 17 16 15 14 13   10 9 8 7 6 5 4 3 2 1

Project management, design, and composition by Steven Hiatt / Hiatt & Dragon, San Francisco   Copyediting: Steven Hiatt   Proofreading: Tom Hassett
Cover Design: Barbara Haines

This book is dedicated to the many courageous patients and entrepreneurs in developing countries who have helped us see the possibilities that lie within everyone, regardless of external circumstances. They have inspired us and created impacts on our lives. It is our hope that through *Pharmacy on a Bicycle* we may do the same for others.

Contents

Preface

Pharmacy on a Bicycle highlights the impact that can be created in global health when diverse groups of innovative and entrepreneurial people come together to achieve a common goal. This book was created in the same way, with different people with diverse perspectives from various parts of the world coming together for a shared and higher purpose.

As authors, we have very different backgrounds, education, and experience—a perfect combination to engage in this project. Marc has been a business school professor for most of his career with extensive work in both the for-profit and not-for-profit sectors. He has written books on innovation, governance, and accountability along with corporate sustainability and social, environmental, and economic impacts. He teaches a class called "Commercializing Technology in Developing Countries" that focuses on health. He takes his students to Rwanda or Liberia each year to find commercial solutions to the health and education challenges of the global poor.

Eric is a physician with an MBA who combines his training in health and business to help solve global health challenges. He leads global health at the George W. Bush Institute, a presidential center designed to move ideas into action, and is a professor of global health at Southern Methodist University. He has taught health care management, consulted for health ministries, and created and directed nongovernmental organizations and research centers in Africa, Latin America, and the United States.

We came together combining our joint competencies, education, and experience to try to alleviate suffering and poverty. Although our skills are quite different, we both recognized that the solutions to global health problems are less about the need for new scientific discoveries and more about logistics, dissemination, and implementation of *what we already know*. We can cure many of these diseases, yet people throughout the world still are dying.

Though *Pharmacy on a Bicycle* represents our own views and we are solely responsible for its content, we are indebted to many people who have worked hard to help the higher purpose of this book to save lives. We would especially like to thank our research and editing team, including our research and production manager Suraj Patel (George W. Bush Institute) and editor Troy Camplin, as well as research assistants Amit Suneja and Sneha Rao (Rice University), Tara Stevenson, Carina Heckert and Jessica Lott (Southern Methodist University), and Bryan Erickson and Devi Nair (Harvard University). In addition, we would like to thank health policy consultant Sharif Sawires for his scientific contributions and valuable insights. The hard work and dedication of this team cannot be overstated.

We are also incredibly grateful to many colleagues and friends for conversations on multiple continents over the years in which we've discussed and debated some of the ideas presented in this book, including Ahmed Abajobir, Jan Agosti, Ricardo Araya, Jerry Bender, Joan Benson, Trista Bingham, Deborah Birx, Kerri Briggs, Barbara P. Bush, Lisa Carty, David Chard, Karen G. Cheng, Thomas J. Coates, Pamela Collins, Cynthia Davis, Mark Dybul, Freddy Ford, Christopher H. Fox, Catherine Freeman, Gus Gill, Mike Grillo, Charles Hilliard, Jon Huggett, Brooke Jenkins, Jose

Jeronimo, Wilbert Jordan, David Kanouse, Sharon Kapambwe, Jim Yong Kim, John Kraemer, Lejeune Lockett, Anne MacDonald, Elizabeth Marum, Larry Marum, Katrina McGhee, Phil Meyer, Kristie Mikus, Brendan Miniter, Mulindi Muanahamuntu, Charles Murego, Suku Nair, Maria Oden, Doyin Oluwole, Dan Ortiz, Allan Pamba, Groesbeck Parham, Nia Parson, Vikram Patel, Willo Pequenat, Rebecca Richards-Kortum, British Robinson, Mary Jane Rotheram, Amanda Schnetzer, Carolyn Smith-Morris, Julia Taylor, Gina Tesla, Edwin Tomyoy, Charity Wallace, Jane Wantgui, and Gail E. Wyatt. At times, a simple question or comment or quizzical look from one of them would prompt us to think deeper, and we discovered new insights in the process.

We are appreciative of the many students, staff, faculty, and administration of Southern Methodist University, Rice University, Charles Drew University of Medicine and Science, and the George W. Bush Institute who have supported our efforts over the years. And we sincerely appreciate the Starkey Hearing Foundation, Bill and Melinda Gates Foundation, National Breast Cancer Foundation, Sharad Lakhanpal, and Gregg Mamikunian, as well as the Bush Institute development team, for their generous support of global health at the Bush Institute, which allowed Eric the time to research and write this book; and Rice University, for support of Marc's research and teaching activities in social entrepreneurship in developing countries.

Eric would particularly like to thank President George W. Bush and Mrs. Laura Bush for their leadership in global health and their encouragement and support of his global health efforts; and Mark Langdale and James K. Glassman for their leadership at the George W. Bush Presidential Center and Institute and support of his efforts as well.

We are grateful to Neal Maillet and the terrific team at Berrett-Koehler Publishers, whose efforts greatly improved this book.

And finally, we are particularly grateful to our families, who, whether in person or in spirit, have unconditionally loved, supported, and inspired us. In particular, we thank Marc's family: Joanne

Epstein, the Firestone family (Simcha, Debbie, Emily, Noah, and Maya), and the Zivley family (Scott, Judy, Amanda, and Katie). As well as Eric's family: Randy Kender, Bryan Erickson, Henry, Lorraine, Diana, Donald and Lorrie Bing, and Cora Bailey. This book and our lives are stronger and more complete because of them.

Eric G. Bing
Dallas, Texas

Marc J. Epstein
Houston, Texas
February 2013

Introduction

Why Pharmacy on a Bicycle

Dawa paced in front of Pemba's door, trying to hide his concern.[1] He had run out of his medication, and Pemba had been kind enough to share his. Both men had been told to never stop taking their medications because HIV was a virus that could quickly develop resistance, and then the drugs would no longer work. Now Pemba was beginning to run out of his supply as well.

Dawa and Pemba were running low on medicine because a *bandh,* or strike, was making it impossible to get to the pharmacy. In Nepal, during a *bandh,* it was wise to avoid going out in a car, because if you did, you could get your tires slashed, your windows broken, or your vehicle set on fire. The *bandh* was in its second week, and the men had nowhere to turn once their medications ran out.

Crises stimulate action. In dire straits, we become innovative and entrepreneurial. Which is what happened in this case. The Saath-Saath Project, a local HIV program, partnered with a hospital and some community health workers to create a pharmacy-on-a-bicycle brigade. If the patients couldn't go to the pharmacy, then the pharmacy would go to them.

It was a risky proposition. Would the *bandh* enforcers respect the riders' mission? Nobody knew. But lives were at stake. That is why Suraj, a community health worker and person living with HIV himself, was one of the first to volunteer. Suraj set out early in the morning after loading his satchel with medications. By midday his pharmacy on a bicycle reached Dawa and Pemba—right before their pills ran out. Because of quick thinking, a partnership, and a bicycle, Dawa and Pemba didn't miss a single dose. This simple solution may have saved their lives.

If all we had to worry about was the occasional strike, most of our problems in global health would be solved. But a *bandh* that lasted thirty-two days only exacerbated Nepal's problems of deep poverty and a population living in hard-to-reach areas. Such problems are found in many developing countries, and regardless of whether they are caused by instability, conflict, geography or cost, they make it difficult to bridge the "final mile" in global health.

Over the last few decades the authors have examined health care in remote rural and dense urban settings across a variety of low- and middle-income countries in Africa, Asia, and Latin America. Some countries were stable, others were in civil war. We have spoken with presidents and health ministers, tribal leaders and CEOs, and patients and their families. We have worked alongside dedicated and compassionate clinicians—doctors, nurses, community workers, and traditional healers—and we have consulted with governments, businesses, NGOs, and donors. We have examined health care from a variety of perspectives, and we always reach the same conclusion:

Millions are dying of diseases we can easily and inexpensively prevent, diagnose, and treat.

Pharmacy on a Bicycle is a bold yet practical approach to alleviating problems in global health and poverty. Fortunately, we are not starting from scratch. There are many examples of successful programs that are already saving lives. We need to leverage these innovative and entrepreneurial solutions and create even more to save lives by increasing access, use, and quality of care, while reducing costs.

In *Pharmacy on a Bicycle*, we show how we can save lives while saving money through a seven-point approach we call *IMPACTS* (Figure 1). Here are the key components:

Figure 1 The *IMPACTS* Approach

 Stimulating *Innovation and Entrepreneurship* to develop new solutions and reach populations in need in sustainable ways.

 Maximizing Efficiency and Effectiveness to deliver quality products and services at reduced costs.

 Partner Coordination to stimulate cross-sector collaboration and coordinate complementary roles.

 Accountability that encompasses defining goals and targets and monitoring success.

 Creating Demand for products and services.

 Task Shifting to lower-level providers and to new settings to reach and serve more people at lower cost.

 Scaling up programs to save even more lives.

Implementing the *IMPACTS* approach will help bring care to those who need it most.

How to Use This Book

This is a book about taking health care the last mile—sometimes quite literally—to a place that's accessible, in a way that's acceptable, and at a cost that's affordable.

In other words, this book is about *solutions*.

There are people and organizations already doing many things that work. Now we need to scale those models to reach the masses of people who deserve quality health care. What works may come from governments, NGOs, businesses, or donors. All are part of the solution to the problems we face, and all have a role to play.

- *Government.* Governments can help create an environment, supported by sound policies, regulations, and resources, where basic, high-quality health care is expected. Ministries of health are the backbones of strong national health systems upon which services are built. Local and national government leadership and commitment are essential for success and financial sustainability.

- *Nongovernmental Organizations.* NGOs, including faith-based organizations, have long provided essential health care, social services, and advocacy in developing countries throughout the world. They are critical to providing quality care in diverse and hard-to-reach communities.

- *Businesses.* For-profit businesses offer not just resources but models of efficiency, innovation, entrepreneurship, and distribution: ways to create demand and reduce costs. In addition, local businesses, along with microenterprises, are often created and based within communities, and owners understand the local culture and needs. Microenterprises in health care, which include small clinics and pharmacies, can help distribute services and products to those in need. So too can traditional healers and traditional birth attendants, particularly in rural areas. For a variety of reasons, these smaller providers and traditional sectors may not be integrated into formal health care systems. But when given

appropriate training, support, and oversight, they can help
us complete the final mile.

- *Donors.* International agencies, foreign governments, and
  foundations provide essential financial and technical support
  to country-led health programs. Such donors are essential
  to enable governments and local implementers to provide
  needed services.

Innovative partnerships that bring these sectors together can
help save more lives. In addition, the approaches used by these
sectors overlap and complement each other as they grow and
evolve. For example:

- Effective governments in many developing countries are now
  adopting sound internal business strategies and practices to
  manage public resources to deliver health services.
- Many NGOs in low- and middle-income countries operate
  like businesses to ensure that their resources are effectively
  used and have real impact. Some NGOs are even creating
  for-profit spinoffs to enhance their chances of creating financially sustainable programs.
- Businesses, large and small, seek not only to be financially
  profitable, but also to create social good in the countries
  where they work. This approach goes beyond corporate social responsibility—it is part of their business model.
- Donors are increasingly requiring recipients to reduce costs,
  demonstrate impact, and achieve greater financial sustainability once support ends.

These new, blended approaches are also helping to change the
perceptions of target populations from beneficiaries to customers. This change in orientation recognizes that a patient is a customer and that the customer is in charge. All people, regardless
of income, are customers of health products and services. When
customers perceive little value in or encounter barriers to using a

health product or service, it is likely that they won't use it—even if it's free and potentially lifesaving. Our job, therefore, is to find innovative and entrepreneurial ways to motivate customers to use health products and services that can save their lives.

Pharmacy on a Bicycle is filled with practical examples of innovative and entrepreneurial solutions to health care delivery in a wide variety of settings in developing countries. While this book focuses on low- and middle-income countries, many elements are readily applicable to populations in higher-income countries as well.[2] Innovation is much more than discovery; entrepreneurship is much more than maximizing profits. The innovator creates solutions. And the entrepreneur finds efficient, effective, and economical ways to get solutions to customers.

We encourage those readers who develop or manage health programs to read *Pharmacy on a Bicycle* with an entrepreneurial lens and find ways you and others can take some of these ideas to the next level to deliver health services. Regardless of your specialty, population, or setting, you may see a solution to a problem you're working on, even if it was developed to combat a different disease, for a different population, under different circumstances, or in a different country.

If you see a model that might work for you, *try it*. If you see a model that, with some modifications, might serve your needs, then *change it*. If you see several models you think could work well together, then *combine them*. And as with any other model, new or old, monitor it regularly and evaluate it periodically to ensure that it's producing the intended impact.

Regardless of your reason for reading this book, in presenting the *IMPACTS* approach and spotlighting successful real-world applications of its core points, we hope to activate your inner innovator and entrepreneur so that you can see existing solutions or create new solutions to the challenges you face.

We have divided the book into three sections:

Part 1: The Prescription includes four chapters that deal with the basics—the essential ingredients, the model, and the core elements of our approach.

- **Chapter 1** provides an overview of the issues, the *IMPACTS* approach, and the model that describes how to save millions of lives and billions of dollars in global health care.
- **Chapter 2** describes the roles innovation and entrepreneurship play in improving global health.
- **Chapter 3** describes how task shifting, maximizing efficiency and effectiveness, creating demand, and focusing on accountability can better deliver health services and products and improve outcomes.
- **Chapter 4** provides an overview of how to scale up interventions and the importance of coordinating the roles of partners to reach more people.

Part 2: IMPACTS in Motion provides three chapters of real-world applications of each point of the *IMPACTS* approach and how they are being used with different diseases and in different settings.
- **Chapter 5** focuses on applications in maternal and child health issues.
- **Chapter 6** reviews applications in some infectious diseases.
- **Chapter 7** discusses issues and applications to some noncommunicable diseases.

Part 3: Moving Forward includes two chapters that show you how to move to the next steps in order to better deliver quality care to those who need it most.
- **Chapter 8** discusses the importance of priorities, planning, and monitoring progress to save lives.
- **Chapter 9** explains how organizations can influence their settings and environments to improve impact and provides recommendations for future steps.

Each chapter in Parts 1 and 2 is concluded by "Food for Thought" questions designed to help you discover ways to apply the concepts to your own setting. At the end of the book, you will find information on www.pharmacyonabicycle.com, a website where you can find and share additional innovative and entrepreneurial solutions for improving global health and alleviating poverty.

The organization of *Pharmacy on a Bicycle* will make it easy to find the important foundational components (Part 1: The Prescription), real-world applications (Part 2: *IMPACTS* in Motion), and recommendations for planning and next steps (Part 3: Moving Forward). How you choose to approach and combine them is up to you.

Now is the time. We can save lives by bringing low-cost, quality care to those who need it most, regardless of whether it is delivered by a community health worker on foot, by a doctor using telemedicine, by a nurse on a mobile phone, or by a pharmacy on a bicycle.

Every great dream begins with a dreamer. Always remember, you have within you the strength, the patience, and the passion to reach for the stars to change the world.

Harriet Tubman
Courageous Humanitarian,
Abolitionist (1820–1913)

Part 1
The Prescription

1

Saving Millions

Every four minutes over fifty children under the age of five die. That's almost 7 million children per year. And nearly one-third of these children die within the first month of life. In the same four minutes, two mothers lose their lives while trying to give birth to a child. And *nearly every time* these tragedies occur, they are happening in a developing country.[1]

A Challenge We Can Solve

Pharmacy on a Bicycle is about innovative and entrepreneurial solutions to these global health calamities and about how all organizations —governments, NGOs, businesses, and donors—can use the solutions to maximum effect.

Nearly 7 million children could be saved by simple things such as providing a mother with prenatal care and encouraging her to give her baby breast milk and clean water, get postnatal care, and receive appropriate vaccinations.[2] A small dose of daily aspirin might reduce risk of death from heart attack or stroke and simultaneously cut the risk for some cancers.[3]

Deaths from cervical cancer could be cut with a simple drop of vinegar applied to the cervix to help a clinician identify potentially cancerous cells,[4] kids could learn better with inexpensive glasses,[5] and depression could be relieved, or a suicide prevented, by talking with a trained lay counselor.[6]

If It's So Simple, Why Aren't We Doing It?

So why are people in developing countries continuing to die from diseases we rarely see in developed countries? Most poor outcomes are caused not by lack of effective medicines or medical know-how. The ability to prevent and treat many of these diseases inexpensively has been available for a very long time. But getting the right remedies to the right people in the locations where they are needed, in a way they will use them, and at a cost they can afford is continually a challenge.

This is not a scientific problem. It's a *business challenge*.

Solving the Puzzle

In order to save lives in global health, we need to increase health care access, use, and quality of services—all while reducing costs. These are all critical pieces of the puzzle (Figure 2). Fortunately, the tremendous progress made in these areas during the past two decades gives us reason to be hopeful.

Over the past twenty years, deaths for pregnant mothers and for children under five years old have plummeted by nearly 30 percent and 40 percent, respectively.[7] More than 8 million people with HIV are now receiving life-sustaining antiretroviral drugs (ARVs), a twentyfold increase from just a decade ago.[8]

This progress is largely a result of business-oriented approaches to providing and using foreign health assistance. These approaches have focused on country ownership of

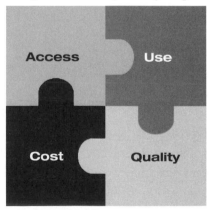

Figure 2 Solving the Health Care Puzzle

problems and solutions, clear objectives, specific targets, a framework for accountability, and a commitment to measurable results. These successful efforts have been supported by better coordination among donors, resulting in a more than fourfold increase in health-related development assistance.

The President's Emergency Program for AIDS Relief (PEPFAR), created by President George W. Bush in 2003 and continued by President Barack Obama, has committed $45 billion to HIV prevention, treatment, and care since it began. PEPFAR is complemented by the Global Fund to Fight AIDS, Tuberculosis, and Malaria. The Global Fund is a multinational effort supported by a large number of countries and private donors, which have provided $32 billion to support health care programs in developing countries. These institutions have helped jump-start global efforts to combat HIV/AIDS. Similar initiatives have helped curtail malaria, reduce maternal and child deaths, and build stronger health systems.[9]

Through strategic alliances, committed partners have not only provided financial resources, but have leveraged their networks and complementary business, technological, and scientific strengths to solve global health problems. Partners have come from a variety of sectors, including governments, international development organizations, foundations, and universities, and they have worked with local organizations and leaders in the communities that are afflicted.

These local partners intimately understand the subtle but critical factors that can mean success or failure of a program or business. Working together they have helped improve access to health services for some populations and conditions, increase the quality of care, and reduce the costs of providing these services.

This progress, coupled with additional technological and business model innovations in global health, helps to make saving lives now even more feasible.

Innovations in Global Health

Mobile Technology

Recent developments in technology, especially mobile devices, can make distributing solutions for global health challenges cheap and easy. It is estimated that in many low-income countries, up to 90 percent of the population has access to a mobile phone.[10] The health care potential of mobile phones is huge, and will become even greater over time.

Effectively using mobile solutions can bring health services to people who need them. Mobile phones are now being used for patient education and awareness, treatment compliance, health care worker training, data collection, disease and epidemic outbreak tracking, and diagnostic and treatment support. These solutions can help increase access, use, and quality, while reducing costs. As a result, mobile technology has the potential to create leapfrog advances in health around the world.

Rapid Diagnostic Tests and Simplified Treatment

New technologies are emerging that allow easier, more effective prevention, diagnosis, and treatment. Rapid diagnostic tests for diseases such as malaria and HIV can be performed in the field, reducing the need for and burden on laboratories and technicians.

Many diagnostic tests require expensive equipment that are typically found only in larger, centralized laboratories, clinics, or hospitals. For most tests, the patient must travel to the testing center. Even after spending the time and money to make the journey and see a provider, the visit may not help them. Equipment may be broken, or there could be long backlogs of tests to be performed. Rapid diagnostics can remove these time-consuming delays and provide point-of-care decisions, improving health care access for rural communities. Further, combining medications into a single tablet whenever possible simplifies medication use and can improve medication adherence.[11] By simplifying treatments we can make it more likely that people will actually use the treatment, and that they will use it properly.

Franchises

An additional business approach that provides opportunities to scale global health effectively is the development of health franchises and networks. Franchises can standardize care at local clinics and pharmacies and help reduce costs through purchasing in bulk, improving supply chain management, and increasing quality with other systems of monitoring and support. When run by local entrepreneurs who know community needs, franchises can create local demand. Franchising and networks provide a solution that harnesses this entrepreneurial base while addressing many of the quality challenges faced by independently operated health clinics and pharmacies.

Challenges and Solutions

While there have been notable successes in global health, some very significant challenges remain:

- *Lack of Basic Health Care.* Most people in developing countries, particularly in rural settings, still don't have access to basic health care and are dying of preventable causes.
- *Fragmented Care.* Some of the successful outcomes in global health have benefited from focused attention and commitment to combatting specific diseases, such as AIDS, malaria, diarrhea, pneumonia, and smallpox. Efforts to prevent and treat these various diseases are often provided by different health systems and settings and by different caregivers, leading to care that is fragmented and that may not be sustainable over time. For example, successfully preventing HIV transmission from mother to child has little meaning if the child soon dies from malaria, pneumonia, or diarrhea— diseases that are not the focus of the HIV sector. Building upon the successful disease-specific systems and integrating care between sectors may help expand distribution of health products and services for more people, in more settings, more efficiently.[12]

- *Financial Sustainability.* There is an urgent need to create financially sustainable health programs, organizations, businesses and systems to ensure long-term impact on global health. As traditional donor countries' economies have struggled, willingness to maintain consistent levels of assistance has become more tenuous.[13] Donors, like host countries and communities, want financially sustainable health solutions rather than temporary or quick fixes.

We can build upon these successes now to create significant impacts in health.

The *IMPACTS* Approach

Our *IMPACTS* approach (Figure 3) builds upon global health and management lessons learned in practice over the last three decades and integrates the key points that can make significant improvements in global health. The seven-point *IMPACTS* approach can help increase health care service distribution in ways that enhance access, use, and quality of care, while lowering costs. Though our focus is on health in low- and middle-income countries, the *IMPACTS* approach has application to higher-income countries whose most vulnerable populations can also fall through the gaps of overburdened health care systems.

| I | Innovation & Entrepreneurship |

Innovation and entrepreneurship are foundational to the *IMPACTS* approach. Innovation is the introduction of new, better ways of doing things. It can involve the creation of more effective processes, services, and products, as well as new technologies. Entrepreneurs are not just creators of new businesses, they are discoverers of opportunities and they can be found in all organizations, including governments, NGOs, businesses, and donor groups. In the context of global health care in low- and middle-income settings, entrepreneurs can find ways to get health products and ser-

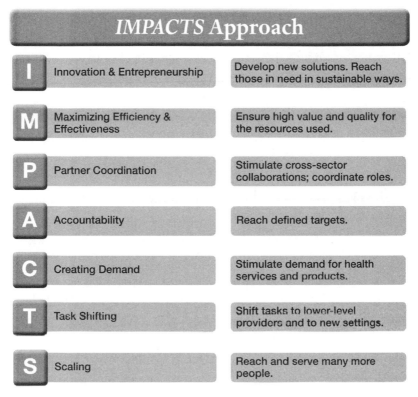

Figure 3 The *IMPACTS* Approach

vices to at-risk populations in ways they desire and at a cost that is financially sustainable.

Ongoing innovation and entrepreneurship is essential to continually finding ways to increase access to and use of services, while improving quality and lowering costs.

M Maximizing Efficiency & Effectiveness

To improve access and reduce costs, it is important to maximize the efficiency with which products and services are produced and delivered. The more efficient a process is, the fewer resources that are required to produce and deliver it. Maximizing efficiency goes hand in hand with maximizing the effectiveness (quality) of the product or service. Efficient and effective health services and products are key in global health.

For example, Aravind Eye Center, a network of specialized eye hospitals in India, uses processes to simultaneously maximize efficiency and effectiveness. The doctors perform thirty to forty surgeries per day by providing unequaled attention to processes. Assistants prepare patients for surgery, and when one patient is finished, another is already in the room, waiting to begin.[14] The high volume of efficient surgeries reduces costs, improves surgeons' skills, and enhances the quality of care they can provide.

P Partner Coordination

Health care in developing countries relies on both the public and private sectors. Even in developing countries there is a private sector for health that includes not only businesses and NGOs, but also traditional health providers, birth attendants, and small clinical practices. In fact, half of all health care expenditures in Africa goes to the private sector.[15]

Unfortunately, in many developing countries, the public and private sectors are often poorly coordinated and regulated, resulting in gaps in services, lost opportunities, poor quality, and unsustainable systems. Like their wealthier counterparts, developing countries need strong public and private sectors that are supported, integrated, and regulated so health care is cost-effective, financially sustainable, safe, trusted, and accessible to the people who need it. Better coordination can help reduce gaps and redundancies among competing programs.

Partner coordination can be done on a large scale by a government or on a smaller scale by a local entrepreneur. For example, VisionSpring, a nonprofit organization, uses local entrepreneurs to sell low-cost eyeglasses to the poor on three continents. These entrepreneurs create partnerships with schools and businesses to provide inexpensive glasses so that students and workers can see better and be more productive.[16] These partnerships benefit everyone, the individuals, the entrepreneurs, and the schools, businesses, and communities in which they live.

Accountability

Accountability measures let us know what works and what needs to be improved. The tools we now have for ongoing public health monitoring are considerably more accurate than those available just a few years ago. They enable earlier detection and the opportunity for more rapid effective responses. When something isn't working, we can identify problems faster and make quick adjustments. Using these tools, global health programs can more effectively establish accountability based on specific measurable goals combined with regular monitoring. This is applicable to all sectors involved: governments, nonprofits, businesses, and donors.

C Creating Demand

Demand for a product or service can increase when people are knowledgeable about it and believe they will benefit from using it, and when it is culturally and socially supported. Making health products or services highly available without also creating demand for them is as futile to improving health outcomes as creating high demand while ignoring availability, accessibility, and affordability. For example, insecticide-treated mosquito nets are widely known to prevent malaria, but in some communities they were not used because a white net seemed to resemble a funeral shroud.[17] It was only by providing green or blue nets that demand was created in some places. This is quite understandable. Would you put a coffin in your bedroom and sleep in it at night if someone told you that it would reduce your risk of getting cancer?

Stimulating interest and creating demand for services, as well as creating incentives for clinicians and community workers, is critically important to providing services in developing countries. When the government of Rwanda provided nonmonetary incentives to both pregnant women and community health workers to increase the use of health services, prenatal visits shot up by over 85 percent in just nine months.[18]

A critical way of creating demand is through engagement of influential people to champion a cause, a product, or a service. Some champions may be highly visible, such as a politician, sports figure, or musician. Others, such as village elders or religious leaders, may be less visible but highly influential in local communities and extremely important in creating demand for health care among families and individuals.

T Task Shifting

In task shifting in health, tasks are shifted from doctors to nurses and from nurses to community providers or patients. Tasks can also be shifted from the specialty sector to a nonspecialty sector. Task shifting helps reduce system bottlenecks and costs by increasing the supply of lower-level providers and settings where quality services can be provided (Figure 4).

In many clinical settings, tasks that doctors formerly performed, such as routine prescription of HIV medications, are now done effectively by nurses.[19] Procedures that nurses formerly performed, like contraceptive implants, can be safely done by trained community health workers.[20]

Task shifting can be effective not only for clinical services, but for clinical operations as well. For example, the Ugandan Ministry of Health is working to avoid clinic stock-outs by decentralizing supply management and empowering clinic staff through a program called mTrac.[21] The program allows health workers to notify the National Medical Stores when supplies get low using text messages. In addition, the program allows the Ministry of Health to map real-time facility stocks using data submitted as text messages. As an incentive, staff members who send in results via text message get free airtime on their mobile phones. Through a complementary program, uReport, even community members can engage by anonymously sending a free text message when clinics run out of medications.[22] Task shifting to different providers and settings has also been used to improve access to care for many

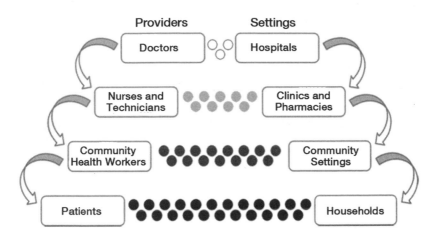

Figure 4 Task Shifting

health conditions, from family planning to clinical depression.[23]

In order to shift tasks as well as to improve quality, tasks must be broken into smaller essential parts, and providers must be trained to execute them well and must be consistently supported and regularly supervised. Simplifying procedures and rules helps ensure fidelity by making it clear what is expected of everyone.

 Scaling

There are many examples in all fields of quite remarkable high-quality innovations that have been developed for small groups of people—a school, health facility, or business. They are terrific, but they benefit only a few. There are also many examples of programs and institutions that have gone to scale and reach large groups of people, but with a relatively low level of quality. To be maximally effective in saving lives, we must take successful, high-quality programs to scale to reach more people.

The components of *IMPACTS* are interrelated and complement one another. For example, efficiencies can be improved by task shifting or better coordination in partner contribution. Improved partner coordination, demand creation, and task shifting can facilitate successful scaling. Likewise, scaling can lead to improved efficiencies and help reach accountability targets. And all of these points rest on a foundation of innovative thinking and entrepreneurial action.

A Global Health Impacts Logic Model

We have developed a logic model to depict how global health organizations can have long-term impact. The logic model provides a clear articulation of an organization's intended impact and the critical activities that drive success (Figure 5). It serves as a visual representation of the relationships among the available resources, necessary activities, and desired results.[24] The logic model helps managers, leaders, and stakeholders understand:

- The causal relationships between the various alternative actions that can be taken
- The impact of these actions on the system, the individual, and the community

By carefully identifying these interrelationships and by establishing relevant performance metrics to measuring success, an organization can improve decision making and inform others, internally and externally, who control or influence resources.

The Global Health Impacts Logic Model describes drivers of global health, the actions managers can take to improve performance and the consequences of those actions on individual and community health. Continual feedback loops are also necessary to allow leaders to evaluate and improve their strategies. The logic model is a general framework that managers should customize to fit their specific needs and environment.

A fundamental component of this model is the distinction between short-term outputs, medium-term outcomes, and long-term results (impacts). Outputs and outcomes must be carefully defined and monitored to determine the effectiveness of processes in place to achieve impacts. Ultimately, program success can be seen in the social and economic effects on the community.

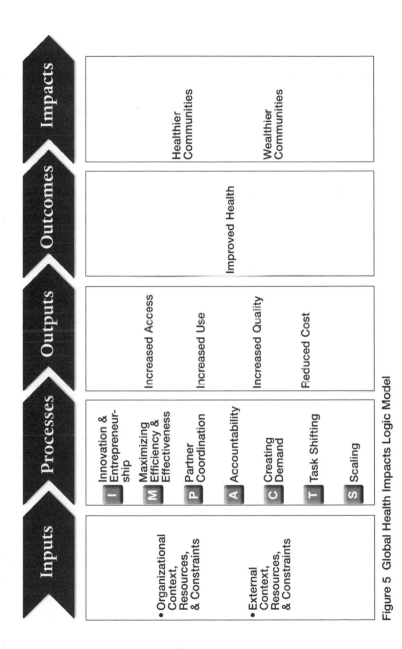

Figure 5 Global Health Impacts Logic Model

Starting Here. Starting Now

Millions are dying of diseases that we can easily and inexpensively prevent, diagnose, and treat. Our challenge in global health is not one of lack of medical know-how. It is that we are not getting the right remedies to the right people, where they need them, in a way that they will use them, and at a cost they can afford. We can reach and save millions simply by stimulating innovation and entrepreneurship, maximizing efficiency and effectiveness, coordinating our work with partners, being accountable for results, creating demand for health services, shifting tasks to workers and settings to reach more for less cost, and scaling up to reach more. Now is the time to save millions in global health.

Food for Thought

- What are your organization's goals and intended impacts? How do they guide your decisions? How do you share them with others?
- How might you double your impact or the number of people served over the next three years? What obstacles might make this difficult? How might you navigate these obstacles?
- Which three peer organizations are the most innovative or entrepreneurial? What do they do differently than you to encourage innovation and entrepreneurship? If you're not sure, how could you find out?

Appendix: Detailed Components of the Global Health Impacts Logic Model

Inputs

The inputs of the logic model include an organization's internal and external context, resources, and constraints. These guide the decisions of leaders and the processes the organization uses to improve the health of the population. They provide a foundation for understanding the complex factors that leaders should consider when developing programs and making decisions.

Organizational. These inputs include all of the internal contextual factors and resources available. This includes financial capital, personnel, systems, brand recognition, and organizational culture.

External. External inputs significantly affect the choices an organization makes regarding the formulation and implementation of a strategy. These inputs include economic constraints and competing needs, system infrastructure, social and cultural factors, and the business environment, including competition and regulatory guidelines that may vary by country and can change over time.

Processes

After evaluating the inputs and considering the program's goals, leaders can develop the appropriate processes to improve the health of target populations. Our *IMPACTS* approach describes these processes.

The processes put in place for an organization are highly dependent on the inputs and desired impacts. *IMPACTS* elements can be used to leverage system strengths and minimize costs to achieve organizational objectives.

Outputs

The outputs of an organization are the short-term results of the processes in place. In the Global Health Impacts Logic Model, these outputs are related to access, use, quality, and cost. An organization's activities can affect one or more of these outputs.

Access. Improving access means improving the ability of health care services and products to reach those in need. Often, geographic distances and time constraints prevent individuals from receiving lifesaving care and services.

Use. Providing affordable health care that is easily accessible does not guarantee that target populations will actually take advantage of it and make use of the care. It is important that what is being offered is actually used—and to be used, people must believe that its value is greater than its costs, both financial and nonfinancial.

Quality. High-quality products and services are important to improving health. Improved health cannot be achieved with increased access and use alone. Accountability processes must be in place to monitor quality.

Cost. The cost of producing and providing health products and services is a crucial factor in determining whether it will be available or used. Costs of products and services must not be confused with the amount paid by a consumer. Portions of the total costs may be borne by the consumer, the government, NGOs, donors, and/or other entities. By reducing costs, regardless of who pays for it, you increase the likelihood that a product or service will be accessible, used, and financially sustainable over time.

Outcomes

By improving the outputs (increasing access, use, and quality, and decreasing cost), organizations are more likely to improve health outcomes.

Impacts

The ultimate goal in global health is to improve the long-term health of the target community. Improved health allows individuals to pursue education, to work, to care for others, and to contribute to society. Improved health has benefits to society far beyond health.

2

Ideas in Action: Innovation and Entrepreneurship

In much of Africa, Asia, and Latin America, there are few health workers, pharmacies, or clinics, particularly in rural areas, making it difficult to deliver inexpensive, high-quality health care to those most in need. When people in these regions get sick, they often get little care or no care at all.

People with the least access to the formal care system typically rely on informal health care, such as folk remedies from family, friends, or traditional healers, which may be ineffective. Others may travel by foot or even be pushed in a wheelbarrow many miles to seek health care in a larger village. Many who do eventually receive skilled medical attention arrive too late to be saved. Too often, they simply die at home or in transit. Requiring poor people without transportation to come to the few places they can get affordable, quality care is killing them: we must bring quality care to them.

Developing innovative ways to bring care to these people in need is what motivates groups of students and faculty at Rice University in Houston, Texas. They work to address health needs in developing countries, whose low-resource environments have little financial capital, limited human capital, poor roads, inter-

mittent power supplies, and few other typically needed resources. One group of innovators is working to develop appropriate
solutions, like a low-cost but effective bubble Continuous Positive Airway Pressure (CPAP) system developed to help infants in
poor countries with respiratory problems breathe more easily.[1]
Another group is working on projects like a low-cost, electricity-
free centrifuge—using a salad spinner, hair combs, and a round
plastic container—that can test up to thirty blood samples at once
so community outreach workers can accurately diagnose anemia.[2]

These unmet needs in global health are also what motivate
innovators at PATH, an international nonprofit organization, to
focus on "transforming global health through innovation." With
over a thousand staff skilled in business, marketing, science, technology, development, and other critical fields, and operational in
over seventy countries, PATH works to improve global health by
advancing technology, strengthening systems, and encouraging
healthy behaviors.[3]

Both Rice and PATH recognize that global health challenges
require business and technology innovation and entrepreneurial
solutions. Indeed, the limitations of developing countries, coupled
with tremendous opportunities to create sustainable impacts, help
drive these health entrepreneurs to be particularly creative and innovative. But while technological solutions are valuable, to make
them effective organizations must address a challenge at least as
difficult: successfully distributing these innovative health technologies to the customers who need them by solving issues related
to what in business is typically called "the last mile." To this end,
business model innovations are also needed. Getting products
and services to customers in need is a significant logistics challenge. However, businesses do this all the time. Regardless of the
remoteness of a given location, you can almost always find products like a cell phone or Coke that, incidentally, people are buying.

Business model innovation can be developed and implemented
by all sectors: governments, NGOs, businesses, and donors. And
these same organizations need to be more entrepreneurial to actu-

ally make it all work. That is why the first point in the *IMPACTS* approach focuses on innovation and entrepreneurship.

According to Peter Drucker, a writer and consultant some consider to be the inventor of modern management, "Innovation is the effort to create purposeful focused change in an enterprise's economic or social potential."[4] Innovation is crucial for every organization to thrive. But in-

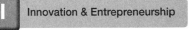

Innovation & Entrepreneurship

novation is required not just within organizations, but in the ways we organize people to accomplish goals, including the delivery of health care. Innovation requires risk-taking. We often cannot know what will work unless we try.

James M. Kilts, former chairman and CEO of The Gillette Company (now part of Procter & Gamble), observed, "You need to encourage risk-taking. One of the themes in our company is to remember that the opposite of success is not failure but inertia."[5] That puts innovation in the right context: it is critical for growth among all sectors—as important to a microentrepreneur in India, a faith-based organization in Nigeria, and the government of Brazil as it is to a multinational corporation in Japan. Without innovation, organizations stall—and consequently collapse.

Innovation is the key point in achieving progress, regardless of sector or setting. Organizations cannot improve outcomes through cost reduction and reengineering alone. Exactly what type of growth innovation creates depends on the needs of the organization, the internal and external environment, and its competencies. For corporations and microentrepreneurs, innovation can result in revenue growth, a stronger bottom line, improved consumer relationships, more motivated employees, enhanced partnership performance, and increased competitive advantage. For governments and NGOs, it can be all of the above, increasing social impact by successfully meeting the needs of their customers—the communities they serve.

One of the most common misconceptions is that innovation is primarily, if not exclusively, about changing technology.[6] Mention innovation to many business, NGO, or government leaders and they envision research and development labs where engineers and scientists are creating the next new technology. However, innovation applies to more than technology; it also involves changes in processes and organizational designs. This can include new rules and regulations, clever ways of bringing products or services to people, novel ideas that change the culture, and new attitudes and values that change people's behaviors, among other things.

Sometimes new or modified regulations and policies can be the critical element in solving a seemingly insurmountable problem, such as seatbelt laws and speed limits to reduce traffic fatalities. Sometimes there is a need to educate people to create demand for products, services, or procedures (such as male circumcision to reduce HIV transmission) that can save lives. Sometimes business models need to change to create efficiencies and become more successful in getting things to the people who need them.

Smart organizations include their customers in the innovation process because customers know the barriers they face and the solutions that will work within their environment, culture, and lives. Often customers are included at the end of the process to see if the innovation was successful, when in actuality they may hold the key to creating innovations that work.

High-performing organizations innovate by designing new business models and improving technologies.[7] Rarely does a technology change occur without also causing a change in management processes. The reverse is also true. Technology and business model innovations go together and should be thought of and implemented as a whole.

While change is critical, it is by no means easy to initiate, attain, or sustain—as anyone who has tried to lose weight and keep it off can attest. There will often be interpersonal, social, organizational, or political opposition to new technologies or business model innovations. Change, even when necessary and possibly lifesaving, is not always welcomed. And the larger the organization is, the less nimble and flexible it may be and the less open to change. Regardless of the size of the organization, when something is not working to achieve our intended impact, we need to be willing and empowered to innovate. Innovation may save lives.

Business Model and Technology Innovation

Business model innovation improves the delivery of products and services to consumers. Technology innovation provides new products and delivers services in new ways. Successful organizations combine business model change and technology change to create innovation. In addition, to successfully integrate a robust model of innovation into the business mindset, leaders must balance the business and technology components of innovation.

There are six levers for change—three in the business model and three in technology (Figure 6).[8] Innovation involves changes to one or more of these six points, as we discuss below.

Business Model Innovation

Business models describe how an organization creates, sells, and delivers value to its customers. Business model change can drive health care innovation in three areas.

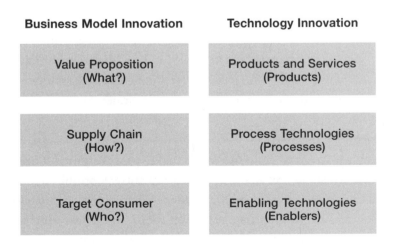

Business Model Innovation	Technology Innovation
Value Proposition (What?)	Products and Services (Products)
Supply Chain (How?)	Process Technologies (Processes)
Target Consumer (Who?)	Enabling Technologies (Enablers)

Figure 6 The Six Levers of Innovation

1. *Value proposition:* what is sold and delivered to the marketplace
Changes in the value proposition of the health product or service—essentially, what you sell (or transfer) and deliver to the
marketplace—may be an entirely new health product or service
or an expanded proposition for an existing offering. This and the
other points apply to governments and nonprofits as much as to
corporations and microentrepreneurs.

2. *Supply chain:* how value (health products or services) is created
and delivered to the marketplace
The second element of innovative business model change is the
supply chain—how value is created and delivered to the mar
ket. Changes to the supply chain are usually "behind-the-scenes"
changes that consumers typically do not see. This type of business model change affects steps along the value chain, including
the way an entity organizes, partners with others, and operates
to produce and deliver health products and services. Innovations
may also come from redefining relationships with suppliers or
from carefully managing relationships with partners whose products and services complement those offered by the organization.

3. *Target consumers:* to whom products and services are delivered
Changes in the target customer segments to whom you provide
products or services usually occur when an organization identifies a segment of consumers who would consider its products or
services valuable, but who it has been unable to reach in terms of
creating demand or effective distribution channels.

Technology Innovation
Sometimes new technologies are a major part of an innovation.
Often, they stand out and attract significant attention. At other
times the new technologies are hidden out of sight and are only
seen by the technical people servicing them. Either way, technology change can fuel innovations in three distinct ways:

1. *Product and service offerings:* what is provided

A change to the health products or services an organization offers—or the introduction of an entirely new product or service—is the most easily recognized type of innovation because consumers see the changes firsthand. While this type of innovation is very important and can have a significant impact on organizational success, it is not the only form of technology innovation.

2. *Process technologies:* how value is provided

When we think about technology innovation, we think about innovation that drives the performance of the products or services the organization offers. Product innovation comes to mind because it quickly translates into functionality that the consumer can value and price. But product innovation is only one application of technology. Changes in the technologies that are integral parts of product manufacturing and service delivery can result in better, faster, and less expensive products and services.[9]

These process technology changes are usually invisible to the consumer, but they are often vital to either reducing the cost or improving the quality of a product.[10] Process technologies also include the materials used in manufacturing, since manufacturing and materials are intimately connected. For service providers, process technologies are those elements that allow the service to be delivered. For products and services, process technologies are an essential part of the innovation equation and often enable cost reduction and quality improvement of existing products or services.

3. *Enabling technologies* that allow value to be provided faster

A third source of technology innovation resides in what we call enabling technology. Rather than changing the functionality of the product or the process, enabling technology allows an organization to execute its strategy much faster and thereby leverage time as a source of competitive advantage. Though the least visible to consumers, changes in enabling technologies, such as information technologies, can be very important because they can help ensure better decision-making and financial management. In health care, mobile phones and telemedicine are enabling technologies that have allowed quality care to reach more people faster.

Three Types of Innovation

A number of innovations, such as purifying water and childhood vaccinations, have revolutionized the way disease is prevented and health care is delivered in developing countries. Other innovations include adapting existing technologies, such as mobile phones, to increase access to care. Understanding these innovations in the context of business model and technology change, but also in the context of incremental versus radical innovations, allows leaders in global health to better understand why some problems have yet to be solved, and helps them discover potentially successful solutions.

Innovations differ widely and thus involve different risks and rewards—and *how* you innovate affects *what* you innovate. It is therefore vital to understand the nature of the change required so the innovation effort can be appropriately managed, funded, and resourced. There are three main kinds of innovation: incremental, semi-radical, and radical, according to one system of thought (Figure 7):[11]

- *Incremental innovation* leads to small improvements in existing health products and organizational processes. Incremental innovation always firmly embraces existing technologies and management structures. Although some elements may change slightly in incremental innovation, most stay unchanged.
- *Semi-radical innovation* leads to substantial change to the business model *or* the technology of an organization. Semi-radical innovations include little or no changes to the elements of one of the innovation drivers—the technology or management.

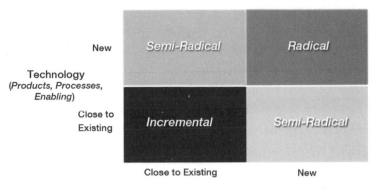

Figure 7 Innovation Matrix

- **Radical innovation** results in new health products or services delivered in new ways. Radical innovations include changes in the technology and business model.

For periods of time an organization (a government agency, an NGO, or a business) can be very successful with only incremental changes in technology. Traditional models of technology change predict relatively long periods of evolution (incremental innovation) punctuated by short periods of revolution (radical innovation).[12] Thus, incremental innovation may be a sustainable strategy for long periods of time, before a revolution shakes an industry or even an entire society.

Incremental Innovation

Incremental innovation is the most common form of innovation in most organizations. Most organizations have created many innovative projects through small changes in management or technology.[13] Incremental innovations are a way to wring as much value as possible from existing products or services without making significant changes requiring major investment.[14] Many management tools are intended to facilitate this type of innovation. For example:

- *Quality control* methods allow health organizations to constantly improve their health products and services.
- *Financial analysis* helps health organizations identify opportunities for cost efficiencies.
- *Market research* that engages communities gains better insight into customer health and needs.
- *Supply chain management* removes activities that do not add value to increase supply chain efficiency.

In some cases, management processes have not been changed or even reviewed for long periods of time and a more dramatic refinement is required—such as restructuring and reengineering.

While incremental innovation may sound like a minor piece in the equation, it is actually the cornerstone. By providing small improvements in technology and management, better products and services can be continually developed and delivered. For example, the introduction of a simple clinical checklist to remind health care workers to do basic things such as washing hands or checking the patient's blood pressure is an incremental innovation that can be lifesaving.[15]

It is easier to work with incremental change than to undertake semi-radical or radical changes. Incremental innovations appear safer and are more comfortable because they are more predictable. Nevertheless, if we want to make significant improvements in global health, we must be willing to complement incremental innovation with more radical innovations.

Semi-Radical Innovation

A semi-radical innovation can provide crucial changes in an organization's ability to improve health outcomes in ways incremental innovation cannot. Semi-radical innovation involves substantial change to the management model or technology of an organization—but not to both.[16] For example, simple, inexpensive text message reminders to people taking antiretroviral medication for

HIV can greatly improve medication adherence.[17] In this case the technology innovation may improve clinical outcomes, but the business model remains the same. Often change in one dimension is linked to change in the other, although the concurrent change may not be as dramatic or disruptive. Semi-radical change in technology may require incremental improvement in the management model, or vice versa.

Another example of semi-radical innovation is franchising in health care. It can improve the quality and reach of health services while reducing financial risk to the entrepreneur. All clinics and pharmacies offer health services and products, but the business model of an independent clinic or pharmacy is very different from that of a franchised one—much as a local mom-and-pop restaurant is different from a franchise of a restaurant chain like McDonald's. Small, local establishments are often widely used because they are familiar and close by. Even when their quality is poor, familiarity and proximity make them compelling forces within the community. Well-run franchises, by using a common format for training, services, and products, paired with internal quality control systems, are able to deliver consistent experiences and quality regardless of location. And by using local entrepreneurs, franchises are able to adapt their services to local preferences while still being able to take advantages of economies of scale.

Blue Star in Bangladesh is just such a franchising network. Franchised by the Social Marketing Corporation, an NGO, the network has 4,000 private health practitioners. These franchisees sign an agreement to offer a specific package of services and to send reports to the franchisor, and in return receive training, on-site quality assurance, technical assistance, and low-cost products. This brings high-quality health care to a larger number of people while providing profits for the franchisees.[18] When managed properly, semi-radical innovation in health has the potential to significantly improve outcomes while minimizing financial risk to the provider.

Radical Innovation

Radical innovation is a simultaneous change to an organization's business model and technology,[19] which usually brings fundamental changes to the field.[20] Such changes have the ability to rewrite the rules of the game in global health.[21] Whether done by governments, NGOs, or businesses, radical innovations may enable them to efficiently and effectively meet critical health and other objectives.

The Jaipur Foot is a radical innovation combining business model and technology advances. Bhagwan Mahaveer Viklang Sahayata Samiti (BMVSS), an Indian NGO, produces this radically innovative artificial lower-limb prosthetic tailored to meet the needs of amputees in low-income regions. Since the poor in India often lack basic things others take for granted, such as chairs to sit on or smooth pavement to walk on, the prosthetic was designed to allow users to squat, sit cross-legged, and work in rugged terrain. In fact, some amputees from high-income countries who have used the Jaipur Foot prefer it over far more expensive prosthetics.

The organization uses local workers to make the prosthetics from locally available resources. Efficient processes, skilled workers, and local raw materials allow them to make these prosthetics in as little as three hours. These efficiencies allow BMVSS to produce the Jaipur Foot for approximately $45 each, in contrast to more traditional products that sell for $10,000 in the U.S. Process efficiencies keep overhead costs down to 4 percent of total operating costs, versus the more typical 20 percent found in many NGOs.[22]

While radical innovation can create game-changing advances in global health, it should be approached with caution.[23] Radical innovations are by nature low-probability investments.[24] Investing in too much radical innovation—based on unrealistic expectations that "the next new thing" will dramatically improve the ability of the organization to save lives—can consume valuable resources that might be better employed on semi-radical or incremental innovations.

While these ideas are clearly relevant to for-profit corporations, they apply to all types of organizations regardless of whether they are businesses, NGOs, or governments. Each type of organization should foster radical, semi-radical, and incremental innovation to create sustainable improvements in health. The key is to effectively maintain a balanced portfolio of innovation (Table 1).

Effectively Integrating Innovations

Innovations in business models and technologies can succeed only if they are effectively integrated into existing systems and communities. Too often global health products and services have been developed with little sensitivity to local skills, culture, people, resources, infrastructure, and other aspects of community life. Global health technologies need to be designed rather than just adapted for use in low-resource environments with few health professionals, low-maintenance expertise, and poor infrastructure. Products should be effective, very low cost, simple to use, and easy to repair.

Enablers of innovation:
- Leadership commitment to supporting ideas outside the current strategy
- Partnerships that provide access to additional resources
- Availability of resources (internal and external) to support game-changing ideas

Blockers of innovation:
- Incentives focused (primarily) on avoiding risk
- Perceived competition and other barriers to entry with existing organizations
- Regulatory policies (such as permitting only physicians to prescribe medications)

Table 1 Comparison of Incremental, Semi-Radical, and Radical Innovation

Type of Innovation	Examples
Incremental • Small innovations to management or technology • Limited risk	**Checklists.** Simple checklist reminders to ensure consistency and completion of all tasks (see chapter 3). **Mobile pharmacy.** Mobile pharmacies to overcome infrastructure and supply-chain challenges to reach remote communities (see Introduction). **Insecticide-treated nets.** Bed nets treated with insecticide to repel mosquitoes and reduce the chances of malaria infection.
Semi-Radical • Substantial innovations in management *or* technology • Moderate risk	**Cipla.** India-based pharmaceutical company that combined ARVs from different companies into a fixed-dose combination pill for HIV, making it easier for patients to adhere to drug regimens. **Mobile Alliance for Maternal Action (MAMA).** Public-private partnership delivering health information to mothers via mobile phones (see chapter 5). **VisionSpring.** Social enterprise using microentrepreneurs to provide low-cost eyeglasses to poor communities (see chapter 8).
Radical • Game-changing innovations in both management *and* technology • Bold commitments on multiple fronts • High risk	**uReport.** Crowd-sourcing technology using mobile phones to enforce transparency and accountability in programs and services (see chapter 4). **Pink Ribbon Red Ribbon.** Public-private partnership combating breast cancer and cervical cancer in Africa by leveraging the President's Emergency Plan for AIDS Relief (PEPFAR) platform (see chapter 7). **GAVI.** Public-private partnership increasing demand and supply of vaccines for children in low-income countries (see chapter 4). **Narayana Hrudayalaya.** Hospital group whose extremely efficient processes enable it to provide cardiac and other surgical procedures with quality comparable to those in the United States, but at less than a tenth of the cost (see chapter 8).

Innovation Critical for Low-Resource Settings

Frugal Innovations

New health technology innovations designed for low-resource environments are sometimes called *frugal innovations*, innovations that fit into an existing environment.[25] Frugal innovations are designed to be very low cost and financially sustainable in a poor community, but still of high quality. Frugal innovation is thus driven by financial and environmental circumstances. Rather than limiting innovative thinking, constraints can actually stimulate innovation by forcing us to be particularly creative, leading to simple, inexpensive, yet effective health solutions. Because of their wealth of local knowledge, innovators who live and work in these environments can best understand what is needed by people in those environments.

Reverse Innovations

Reverse innovations have become of interest in both developing and developed countries and have important implications for each.[26] Instead of stripping existing Western products of their bells and whistles to reduce costs and to meet the more basic needs of developing economies, reverse innovators design the product, service, or process specifically for the developing country. "In community, for community" ideas focused on meeting local needs are the goal. When that hurdle is passed, they can move from community to region to world. In this way health-related products and services developed for low- and middle-income countries can find additional markets.

For example, General Electric created a very-low-cost electrocardiogram (ECG), an instrument designed to detect heart abnormalities by measuring the electrical impulse of the heart, in India for the Indian environment. The machine has a green button for "go" and a red button for "stop," and is easy to use—and it is just as effective at picking up abnormalities as more expensive machines, but at one-sixth the price. GE's low-cost ECG, developed for India, is now marketed globally and is used in over ninety countries.[27]

Table 2   Key Components of Frugal and Reverse Innovation

Type of Innovation	Examples
Frugal • Designs specifically for use in low-source settings • More-with-less philosophy	**Jaipur Foot.** Custom-fit artificial lower-limb prosthetic designed to meet the needs of amputees in low-income regions, which costs $30 to produce compared to $10,000 for traditional prosthetics in the U.S. **LifeStraw.** A point-of-use water filter built into a straw that removes over 99 percent of bacteria and parasites. **Siemens Fetal Heart Monitor.** Low-cost fetal heart monitor using microphones instead of traditional, more expensive ultrasound technology.
Reverse • Innovations developed in low-resource settings that are adopted in high-resource settings	**GE ECG.** Low-cost, portable ECG machine developed for low-income regions that is now used in Europe and other developed countries by physicians with individual practices. **Partners in Health.** A program that improved health outcomes in Rwanda and Haiti using paid community health workers. It is now used in the U.S. with similar improvements.

Some types of frugal innovation, such as an incubator that warms a newborn baby with a simple lightbulb, may not be marketable in developed countries. Nevertheless, both types of innovation are important ways for solving health problems in developing countries that may also be a benefit to the rest of the world (Table 2).

Why Entrepreneurship?

Entrepreneurial attitudes and approaches are critical to successfully developing and implementing breakthrough and incremental innovations. One often-quoted definition by Harvard Business School Professor Howard Stevenson is: "Entrepreneurship is the pursuit of opportunity beyond the resources you currently control."[28] This definition takes into account both the individual and the society in which the individual is embedded.[29] That is, an

entrepreneur sees an opportunity, but will not let a lack of resources prevent him or her from trying to take advantage of that
opportunity. That mindset is what makes such people entrepreneurial.

Though many think of entrepreneurship as primarily focused
on for-profit business activities, it is just as critical and applicable
in governments and NGOs. Both the active pursuit of opportunity
and the gathering of human and financial resources are fundamental to success. And the public-private partnerships important
for significant advances in global health rely on effective collaboration and marshaling of resources.

Social entrepreneurs apply entrepreneurial principles to social
ventures. These can be for-profit or nonprofit as long as they
are a) entrepreneurial and b) organized to achieve desired social, cultural, or environmental goals. Many current advances in
global health are being led by social entrepreneurs in the for-
profit, nonprofit, and government sectors. Many challenges for
entrepreneurial activities in global health exist regardless of sector
in developed and developing nations. Most of these developing
countries have a desperate lack of resources and provide tremendous entrepreneurial opportunities. In some regions of the world,
more than 80 percent of the nonagricultural working population
is active in the informal economy.[30]

Some call these traders "necessity entrepreneurs" rather than
entrepreneurs by choice, since they would often prefer employ-
ment with regular wage. But such jobs are typically scarce, so
people become traders out of necessity. Large proportions of the
population in low-income countries can neither read nor do basic
arithmetic, and there are typically large skills gaps and shortages.
Whether for a government, a business, or an NGO, big or small,
this lack of infrastructure and human capital creates challenges
for those looking to alleviate global health problems more effectively. But solutions are available.

The Role of Microentrepreneurship and Microfinance

In developing countries, most businesses are very small. These operations are referred to as microenterprises and often are run by an individual, possibly supported by relatives or friends. These businesses can be involved in a variety of trades, from farming to selling handicrafts, and they play a huge role in the global economy.[31] Two-fifths of the world's population—some 2.5 billion people—live on the equivalent of $2 per day or less.[32] Microenterprises support many of these people.[33]

Most microentrepreneurs aren't small traders or craftsmen happily operating in local markets. The reality is far more grim. They are often poorly trained but highly entrepreneurial women who exploit every means available to make ends meet for their families. These entrepreneurs are hardworking, resourceful, and ingenious, but their businesses are often weak and stagnant, enabling these women to meet basic needs but falling well short of lifting them out of poverty.

Many microenterprises obtain loans from microfinance institutions. These organizations are critical elements of the financing needed to start a business. Microfinance institutions, which are often structured as NGOs, provide financial services to these poor who can't be served effectively and economically by the formal financial sector. Microfinance can help entrepreneurs improve their economic and social well-being by providing the financial resources needed to start new businesses, expand existing businesses, or diversify into new products and industries. But loans aren't enough by themselves. These entrepreneurs need basic management knowledge and skills to help them grow their businesses. Despite the resourcefulness and ingenuity that allow them to develop and operate their businesses at a subsistence level, these business owners lack the knowledge necessary to move beyond that level.

These entrepreneurs are particularly well positioned to deliver health products and services if they receive appropriate training, since they already operate in rural communities. In some developing countries, such businesses employ more than half of the workforce.[34] They already operate in remote areas, understand the cultural intricacies needed to market products, and have personal connections with their customers. Given the estimated $158 billion market for health products and services in developing countries, there is great potential for health products to provide both income to microentrepreneurs and a service to communities.[35]

Businesses and NGOs that supply financial services to the rural poor have recognized the potential benefits, financially and socially, of their clients selling health products in poor communities.[36] Many have supplied their clients with items to sell to community members: health kits consisting of rudimentary first aid supplies, insecticide-treated mosquito nets (to prevent malaria), and oral rehydration therapy (to treat diarrhea). Entrepreneurs need little training to sell many of these basic health products, except skills as sales representatives; with such training, they can promote and market these products more effectively.

The flow of supplies from larger distributors to smaller distributors can facilitate bulk purchases of supplies at discounted prices. Such discounts would otherwise be unavailable to small distributors. As part of a distribution network, they can pass these savings on to consumers. Cell phones and the Internet can support large and small providers, even in the most rural settings.

By using technology and proven models for product and service delivery, these providers can coordinate their efforts to minimize the cost of improving health care systems in developing countries. Coordination of products and services can also ensure that the lack of physical infrastructure does not prevent health care systems from improving care for the rural poor.

Innovation and Entrepreneurship in Global Health
Innovation in global health also means being able to think outside the paradigm of medicine, doctors, surgery, and clinical advice as the only solutions. It requires entrepreneurial approaches utilizing both technology and business model innovations. First, it means

being able to understand innovative distribution channels that present the opportunity to most effectively distribute resources so the most people get the care they need. This requires recognizing that much of the care needed in developing countries does not require a highly trained, skilled physician. Clinicians, pharmacists, community health workers, microentrepreneurs, traditional healers, and birth attendants can all be taught to deliver many services, reducing costs and increasing effectiveness. Second, it requires acknowledging that much of the low-hanging fruit has remained unpicked not because the benefits are not known, but because transferring and implementing the improvements are quite challenging. Implementing these entrepreneurial approaches can increase access, quality, and use while reducing cost.

Community Health Workers

Community health workers in many countries have been critical to providing resources to low-income settings, particularly in rural areas. These workers are often employees of or volunteers for NGOs or governments and live in the communities where they provide services. They generally receive basic training over a few months and receive ongoing supervision, as well as help linking patients to more highly skilled clinicians. In some countries, such as Rwanda, these workers are selected by the communities in which they will serve. In such roles, community health workers have positions of status or influence in the community, which can serve as a nonfinancial incentive for volunteer programs.

The Ethiopian Ministry of Health created the Health Extension Program to train 35,000 community health workers and deploy them to rural village health posts across the country. The extension workers provide health education, preventative care, and basic family health services. The Health Extension Program shows that community health workers can be used to educate about, distribute, and create demand for health products and services.[37]

A large number of tasks can be easily shifted from hospitals and clinics to these trained workers. One does not need a nursing

degree to distribute condoms and aspirin. Further, trained workers can be given checklists and mobile technologies to facilitate
their distribution efforts.

Traditional Birth Attendants

Given that many women are already using them, traditional birth
attendants can be part of the solution of getting good health
services and medications to those who need them in many rural areas in poor countries. These traditional birth attendants are
already interested and motivated health entrepreneurs serving
their communities. Good clinical skills can be learned regardless
of formal educational background. It would be advantageous in
certain settings to help provide traditional birth attendants with
the necessary skills and products to perform certain tasks and to
certify their quality so those using their services are informed and
protected.

Microentrepreneurs

Microentrepreneurs have financial incentives to serve as both
health educators and distributors: they earn the trust of customers, build demand for products, and earn income. Aligning the
incentives for entrepreneurial success with the goal of increasing
access can help bring early disease prevention and health care services closer to those in need. Microentrepreneurship can provide
a more robust and sustainable model for delivering basic health
care products, education, and services to consumers in developing countries. Encouraging microentrepreneurs to deliver basic
interventions can be cost-effective because they often require little
training and can recycle the money they make back into ordering
more health supplies for their communities.

VisionSpring, a nonprofit that trains entrepreneurs to conduct
vision exams and sell glasses,[38] and Living Goods, a nonprofit enabling women entrepreneurs to go door to door selling health care
products like "Avon ladies,"[39] have shown that by aligning the incentives of the entrepreneur with the goal of improved health care

distribution, organizations can better serve both their customers and their communities. These organizations provide low-income individuals, primarily women, with entrepreneurial opportunities selling basic health products in their local communities.

The microentrepreneurs operate for-profit businesses and therefore have incentives to provide health care products to their community. The programs have also proven to be scalable and financially sustainable. Importantly, they have successfully merged commerce with community service and found replicable success in bringing health care to the poor, and thus have a number of advantages:

- Familiarity with the local culture
- Ability to provide solutions tailored to local needs
- Community trust based on familiarity with the microentrepreneur
- Operating in community setting

However, utilizing microentrepreneurs must be done with caution. Measures must be put in place to maintain quality, whether initiated by the entrepreneur, his or her network or franchise, or a governmental regulatory body. Microentrepreneurs are typically not health professionals, and their limitations may result in problems:

- Limited health care knowledge and skill
- Lack of monitoring by and accountability to central organization with technical expertise
- Need for training in distributing basic health products and in business skills

Despite these limitations, microentrepreneurs can play an important role in preventing and treating basic diseases.

Micropharmacies

Micropharmacies are small pharmacies often set up on the franchise model. They are run by local entrepreneurs, distributing basic health care products and transferring knowledge to community members. They make medicines more accessible to even the poorest, most remote communities.

When medications are appropriately prescribed, they can maintain or restore health. However, if they are improperly prescribed and administered, rates of illness and death can rise, antibiotic-resistant strains of infectious diseases can spread, and community trust in the health care delivery system can diminish. Because medications can sicken and even kill people if not properly administered, it is crucial to ensure that these products are of high quality and are distributed appropriately. Thus, proper training for clinicians and pharmacists is needed. Aligning financial incentives with improving access to basic medications to the poor will strengthen the overall health care delivery system.

To this end, nonprofit social franchises like the HealthStore Foundation have developed distribution systems that make drugs accessible and provide a brand customers can trust.[40] These organizations have successfully franchised pharmacies to for-profit entrepreneurs who serve their communities.

As in other microfranchising programs, pharmacy franchisees own their businesses and earn sustainable income for their families. The franchisor lowers the prices patients pay for pharmaceuticals by purchasing on behalf of all its franchisees and leveraging its larger buying power. Franchisees require prior training on the basic treatment of common illnesses, the pharmacology of commonly sold medications, and details of medication dosage and use. Both these organizations demonstrate the potential of merging commercial and NGO models of health care delivery; their methods should serve as a guide for those looking to scale-up quality drug distribution in developing countries.

Microclinics

Microclinics, such as Child and Family Wellness's network of clinics in Kenya and Rwanda, are small clinics that provide basic medical care, including prevention, diagnosis, and treatment, for a short list of common and preventable diseases. In addition, these clinics make health care accessible to poor communities and minimize opportunity costs associated with traveling to hospitals for basic services. They tend to be staffed by providers, such as community health nurses, who have received formal training to provide appropriate, consistent, high-quality care. Some microclinics also contain micropharmacies and distribute medication. Efforts to align clinicians' profits with the goal of improved delivery have helped microclinics discover efficient ways to bring diagnosis and treatment closer to people in rural areas.

Finding the Better Way

Improving global health requires getting better solutions to people in better ways. To do this, we must be continually innovative and entrepreneurial. By stimulating innovation in our business models and technologies, we can stay ahead of the curve to achieve greater impacts in health. Some of the most innovative models in health are being created in developing countries where constraints and unmet needs can help stimulate, rather than hinder, radical innovation. Such innovation may help create leapfrog advances in health not only in developing countries, but throughout the world. Entrepreneurial solutions must also be fostered in every sector—government, NGO, and business. Health entrepreneurs can help us complete health care delivery to the very last mile and save lives. Engaging, training, and supporting the health entrepreneurs that already exist in these settings, such as traditional birth attendants, community health workers, and other microentrepreneurs, allows them to be part of the solution, and can accelerate success.

Child and Family Wellness Shops:
Franchised Microclinics for the Poor

The CFW network is a franchised network of private clinics in Kenya and Rwanda that lends money to entrepreneurs to help them start CFW microclinics, small clinics that provide treatment for the short list of medical conditions that cause 70 to 90 percent of child morbidity in developing countries. The microclinics provide care and dispense medication through their micropharmacies managed by nurses that are typically located within or close to poor communities for ease of access.

In addition to the main conditions the nurses treat, the microclinics are also authorized to provide a limited set of additional health services to meet community needs and increase the viability of their clinics. These microclinics have proven highly successful and provide an average of approximately $200 per month in profit for the nurses who own and operate them.

Entrepreneurs pay an initial franchise fee to enter the system and to license the CFW brand and systems, and are then supported by business training, startup loans, a secure supply chain of high-quality essential medicines and medical supplies, and assistance with site selection, government regulations, and compliance functions. CFW requires that owners maintain quality standards and uses the combined power of the network to secure favorable prices from suppliers. These microclinics face the market realities of profit and loss, competing as low-cost, high-quality providers.

Quality control is managed by regular inspections of all network microclinics and micropharmacies. Those who fail to pass the strict criteria receive warnings and face potential removal from the network. Both profit/loss and inspections create incentives for the provider to provide high-quality care that patients trust. To strengthen that trust, CFW ensures that trustworthy products are available by overseeing the supply chain of pharmaceuticals. This is particularly important in places where large proportions of medications can be substandard or counterfeit.[41]

Food for Thought

- List three technology or business model innovations that might help your organization increase its impact. Whose buy-in might you need to try them?
- What three organizations in your area have skills that might help you increase impact, for example, in supply chain management, financial controls, training, or marketing? Could they share these skills? What might you offer in return?

3

A Shift in Perspective:
Task Shifting to Save More

Two of the main challenges in global health are that we have too few skilled health care providers and too few settings equipped to care for the large number of people who lack basic care. Right now, training large numbers of more highly skilled doctors or building many more highly specialized hospitals to care for patients is neither feasible nor the highest priority. One solution to closing this health gap is to task-shift health care to lower-skill-level providers and localized settings.

The goal of task shifting is to create system efficiencies, ease bottlenecks, and increase reach while reducing costs of services (Figure 8). It involves delegat- ing responsibilities for specific tasks to other providers or oth- er settings. The focus in task shifting should be on the ability of the provider or setting to perform specific tasks in ways that maintain quality, improve distribution, and reduce costs.

Provider-type task shifting typically shifts tasks from providers at upper levels (doctors and others who are highly specialized) to middle (nurses, midwives, and skilled technicians) and lower levels (community workers, family members, and patients).

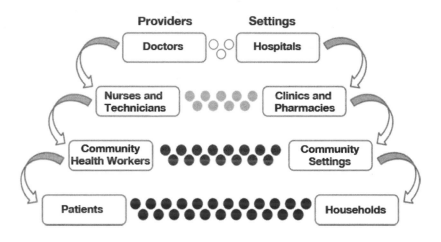

Figure 8 Task Shifting

Health personnel can consume up to 70 percent of recurrent health care expenditures in developing countries, so task shifting to lower-cost health care providers not only can save more lives, it can save money.[1] Since higher-level providers are in short supply and expensive, task shifting improves efficiency by moving tasks that can be performed by others who are available in much greater numbers and may be significantly less expensive.

Task shifting between clinical settings typically shifts tasks from specialized to generalized settings, which may not only include small clinics and pharmacies, but may also include schools, marketplaces, and homes.

Ensuring Success with Task Shifting

A number of system-level changes can help ensure success in task shifting. As tasks are shifted from higher- to lower-level providers, there will be challenges. Lower-level providers need good training and ongoing supervision, monitoring, and support. And as with all clinicians, their newly acquired skills will be lost if they are not used. Good monitoring is needed to ensure that protocols are followed. Such monitoring protects everyone—patients, providers, and supervisors.

If basic support to lower-skilled providers cannot be provided, it may not be in the best interest of the patient to shift tasks. Such basic support includes:

- Appropriate provider training
- Appropriate equipment and supplies to perform new tasks
- Diagnostic algorithms, treatment regimens, and checklists to simplify routine care
- Referral systems in place for advanced care and completed cases
- Ongoing supervision, monitoring, and support

With these essential features in place, task shifting may increase health care access and use while reducing the costs of quality service.

While shifting tasks from specialized health sectors may help scale up care for conditions like HIV or cancer, such a shift will require a level of support similar to that needed when shifting from upper-level to lower-level providers to ensure quality care and good clinical outcomes. Providers in specialized health sectors (for example, HIV or other infectious diseases, cancer, or maternal health) have very specific skill sets developed over years of training and practice. In addition, these sectors often receive more support and funding for training, supplies, and equipment. Such support is often not available in more generalized health sectors.

During the planning stage, all levels of personnel and influential opinion leaders should be engaged in plans to task-shift, so every sector and key stakeholder sees how they will benefit. This may minimize turf battles, professional rivalries, and perceived loss of autonomy and control. Legal or regulatory issues may need to be addressed during planning if regulatory safeguards or restrictions prohibit certain types of tasks from being performed by lower-skilled workers.

E-HealthPoint: Using Telemedicine to Bridge the Health Care Divide

HealthPoint Services India operates a number of E-HealthPoints in rural communities in India. These health units provide families in small villages with clean drinking water and basic health care services. To improve access to quality care, E-HealthPoint units are enabled with telemedicine capabilities, connecting remote communities with licensed doctors and trained health workers. Participating doctors are trained in providing telemedical services and identify cases needing referrals for advanced treatment. To enhance relationships with communities, doctors and health professionals conduct in-person visits periodically. Over a three-year span, E-HealthPoint units provided over 33,000 telemedicine consultations, increasing access to quality health care by supporting community health workers with trained doctors.[3]

Facilitating Task Shifting

Mobile Phones and Telemedicine

Mobile technology can facilitate task shifting by helping supply the kind of quality control necessary for delivery systems to work efficiently. Smartphones can be used to provide checklists for community health workers, track patients, obtain second opinions on complex diagnoses and treatments, and verify drug quality. SMS messaging, for example, can be used to verify if a medication is counterfeit or not.[2]

Telemedicine has greatly facilitated task shifting in some settings. By using telemedicine to provide second opinions and ongoing training, we can side-step limitations due to poor infrastructure, minimize the financial and time costs associated with seeking care far away, and support lower-level health workers to maintain quality care. It may help create trust in the health care delivery system by the patients who will see that though care is provided by lower-skilled providers, they can be "seen" by highly skilled providers when needed. With telemedicine, the same system is in place without the doctor having to be physically present.

More communication is the key to improving health outcomes. The faster and more efficiently we can communicate health information, the better will be our health outcomes.

We must remember, however, that these technologies are facilitators of care, not replacements. There is still a need for face-to-face interactions for good patient care. If used properly, they can help us task-shift to become more efficient and effective and lead to better outcomes.

Bikes and Motorcycles

For task shifting to work well, supply chains must be well managed. Poor infrastructure can place great strains on supply chains serving rural health care providers in developing countries. Having skilled providers to care for the poor is only one part of the solution to bridging the health care gap. These providers must also have appropriate supplies and equipment to do their jobs right.

Clinicians and doctors have donned backpacks and satchels filled with tools to diagnose and treat diseases in rural areas not accessible by car. Some NGOs have tried to move more advanced points of care to the rural poor by using motorcycles and other modes of rapid transportation. Task shifting has the potential to help us reach even more people with even more health care services and products—but only if the workers we are shifting the tasks to can get where they need to go. Vehicles such as motorcycles and bicycles help facilitate the distribution of health care to the poor, and in doing so, help improve health outcomes.

Vehicles can be used to bridge the supply chain gaps that plague many communities in developing countries. Trucks and cars can ensure providers, especially those further down the hierarchy, have consistent access to supply distributors; this becomes especially crucial with illnesses like tuberculosis or HIV/AIDS. Patients with these infections need consistent access to care and treatment to avoid antibiotic and antiretroviral resistance.

Many places can be reached only by small vehicles like motorcycles and bicycles. Riders for Health, an NGO with operations throughout Africa, uses motorcycles to bridge links in strained supply chains in developing countries, allowing health providers to visit more patients, move deeper into rural regions, and respond more rapidly to medical emergencies.[4] A bicycle can cover four times the distance a person can travel on foot and carry five times the weight.[5]

An innovative partnership between World Bicycle Relief, an international NGO started in the aftermath of the tsunami that hit Indonesia, and World Vision, an international faith-based organization with operations in ninety-seven countries, provided 23,000 bicycles to community-based care workers, prevention educators, and orphans with financial support from USAID.[6] Bicycle Empowerment Namibia, an NGO based in Namibia, has built and distributed bicycle ambulances to transport sick and injured people in poor, remote areas to clinics and hospitals.[7]

These bicycle and motorcycle programs work because in addition to ensuring access to the vehicles, the programs also train mechanics to fix them when repairs are needed, creating local jobs.[8] Riders for Health charges health ministries and other NGOs a small fee to train their health care workers in motorcycle repair and to perform regular scheduled maintenance. This model can significantly reduce repair costs and help health care workers consistently reach their patients. Riders for Health enabled the African Infectious Disease Village Clinics (AIDVC), a health care NGO in Kenya, to provide care to more than 90,000 people while operating from a central facility.[9] It travels to bring care to its customers, rather than expecting the customers to travel to them. Together, by being innovative and entrepreneurial, Riders for Health and AIDVC saved lives.

Checklists

Simple clinical checklists can facilitate task shifting and help improve outcomes by ensuring consistency of care by health care workers. One of the areas where checklists have been shown to improve consistency of care is in pregnancy. Although more women in developing countries are delivering in hospital settings, there still has not been an appreciable fall in mortality.

To address this problem, the World Health Organization (WHO) developed the Safe Childbirth Checklist, which covers twenty-nine basic practices such as washing hands, assessing for postpartum bleeding, and breastfeeding within an hour of birth (Table 3). Consistency in doing these very simple practices helps avoid problems such as infections, uncontrolled bleeding, life-threatening hypertension, obstructed labor, and birth asphyxia. Adoption of the Safe Childbirth Checklist has resulted in a 150 percent improvement of adherence to basic procedures in a study conducted at an Indian hospital.[10]

Similarly, another checklist was developed by WHO to increase consistency and reduce complications during any surgery. This checklist covers nineteen basic items applicable to all surgeries.[11] Hospitals that tested the surgical checklist saw an increase in the likelihood of compliance with basic standards of care, resulting in dramatic drops in complications and surgical-site infection. Simple checklists like these can help ensure basic procedures are followed and therefore facilitate the shifting of more tasks to lower-skilled workers.[12]

Effectiveness = High Quality

Ensuring that health care products and services are effective is critical to making strides in global health. There is a constant tension between increasing scale and maintaining quality. High quality often requires more re- 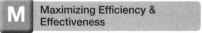 sources, which limits the ability to reduce costs and increase scale; however, poor quality can at best result in no improvement, and at worst it can kill.

Efficiency: The Pros and Cons of Specialized Services

Either general or specialized health services can use task shifting. We need both kinds of services, and we need to know when

Table 3 Selected Components of the WHO Safe Childbirth Checklist

Checklist Item	Response	Qualifying Caption
On admission of the mother to the birth facility		
Does mother need to start antibiotics?	☐ Yes, given ☐ No	Give if temperature ≥ 38°C, foul-smelling vaginal discharge, rupture of membranes >18 hours, OR labor >24 hours
Does mother need to start magnesium sulfate?	☐ Yes, given ☐ No	Give if (1) diastolic blood pressure ≥ 110 mmHg and 3+ proteinuria, OR (2) diastolic blood pressure ≥ 90 mmHg, 2+ proteinuria, and any: severe headache, visual disturbance, OR epigastric pain
Does mother need to start anti-retroviral medicine?	☐ Yes, given ☐ No	Give if mother is HIV+ and in labor
Just before pushing (or before Cesarean)		
Are essential supplies at bedside for mother?	☐ Gloves ☐ Soap and clean water ☐ Oxytocin 10 IU in syringe	Prepare to care for mother immediately after birth: (1) Exclude 2nd baby, (2) Give oxytocin within 1 minute, (3) Controlled cord traction to deliver placenta, (4) Massage uterus after placenta is delivered
Soon after birth (within 1 hour)		
Is mother bleeding too much?	☐ Yes, shout for help ☐ No	If bleeding ≥500 ml, or if ≥250 ml and severely anemic: massage uterus, consider additional uterotonic, start intravenous line, treat cause
Does baby need to start antibiotics?	☐ Yes, given ☐ No	Give if antibiotics were given to mother, or if baby has any: breathing too fast (>60 breaths/min) or too slow (<30 breaths/min), chest in-drawing, grunting, convulsions, no movement on stimulation, OR too cold (temperature <35°C and not rising after warming) or too hot (temperature >38°C)
☐ Started breastfeeding and skin-to-skin contact? (if mother and baby are well)		

Table 3 (Continued)		
Checklist Item	Response	Qualifying Caption
Before discharge		
Is mother's bleed-ing controlled?	☐ Yes ☐ No, treat and delay discharge	
☐ Family planning options dis-cussed and of-fered to mother		
☐ Follow-up arranged for mother and baby		
Source: Spector et al. (2012) "Improving Quality of Care for Maternal and New-born Health: Prospective Pilot Study of the WHO Safe Childbirth Checklist Program."		

to use each (Table 4). General health services provide care for a diverse patient population and can tackle a variety of common diseases. They may allow care to be more tailored to the specific health needs of patients. Within-system referrals and information communication can be streamlined, allowing for better care for those who have multiple problems. However, improving general-ized care and treating a vast array of conditions require a variety of supplies, equipment, and staff skills, potentially creating inef-ficiencies in the system.

Indeed, many of the disadvantages of general care are the ad-vantages of specialized care. A generalist can perform a wider va-riety of routine care, but the specialist may perform a more select group of specialized tasks more efficiently and with higher qual-ity. Specialized care for conditions such as cancer, HIV, and other specific medical conditions may help bring not only the benefits of specialization, but also increase efficiency and lower costs.

To maximize efficiencies, systems must balance the need for efficient specialized care and important generalized care. Through partnerships, as well as a robust private sector, system imbalances

Table 4 Comparison of General Health Care and Specialized Health Care

Type of Health Service	Pros	Cons
General Health Care	• Larger customer base • Economies of scale • Within-system referrals	• Lack of efficiency • Limited expertise
Specialized Health Care	• Efficient • High quality • Develops highly skilled personnel	• Limited scope • Creation of health silos with lack of system integration

can be fixed. If an area has enough cases of a particular condition for a specialized service to create value in the system, it may be profitable to create such a service. Otherwise, it may be more advantageous or profitable to offer generalized services.

It is much more likely that general health care services will be provided by government and that specialized health care services will be provided by for-profits, with NGOs providing both at moderate levels. However, it is possible for any of the three to provide either general or specialized health care. Where there is demand, it will be common to find specialized health care provided by private organizations; where there is less demand for specialized care, it may be more advantageous for private organizations to supply general health care. Indeed, one is much more likely to find more general services in rural areas and more specialized services in urban areas, no matter how wealthy the country.

Elements of both general and specialized health care can be task-shifted to lower level providers, including community outreach workers and microentrepreneurs. Living Goods, an NGO operating in Uganda, and Project Shakti, a program run by Hindustan Unilever, show that networks of microentrepreneurs can distribute a wide variety of general health products. Another organization, VisionSpring, has a network of microentrepreneurs that provide a very specialized set of products, eyeglasses, to low-income communities.

More effective distribution systems help save lives by making disease prevention and medical care more available and accessible to those in need (Table 5). Because global health challenges occur on such a large scale, improved systems need to be cost-effective, scalable, and financially sustainable. To solve the challenge of availability and accessibility, these distribution systems must rely heavily on a sustainable model that integrates and complements governmental and NGO support and facilitates the coordination of products and services. With this approach, increased scale improves cost efficiency, access to products and services, financial sustainability, and societal health and well-being. To treat diseases and prevent their spread, distribution channels must provide education and supplies for treatment and prevention, along with basic, advanced, and emergency treatment.

Education can inform people about many aspects of diseases: how they are transmitted and can be prevented, how health care supplies can help people stay healthy, how to recognize symptoms, and when to seek more intensive diagnosis and treatment. Health supplies—including condoms, sterile delivery kits, soaps, and insecticide-treated bed nets—can help prevent the spread of diseases. Diagnostic tests can help clinicians determine if treatment is necessary and, if so, what type to provide, and thus act to facilitate distribution. Clinicians trained in basic diagnosis and treatment can provide the most care and treatment. Trained providers can safely prescribe basic medications. Each level of the health system provides multiple products and services to address different diseases.

Specialized Hospitals

Hospitals are at the top of the distribution tier. To get more advanced treatment and emergency care, people in low-resource settings need access to hospitals. By shifting some of the burden for basic and routine prevention and care to franchised and other clinics and pharmacies, hospitals can focus their attention on the most complex cases. Doing so relieves stress on the common-

Table 5 Health Service Distribution

Specialized Health Services	Examples
Hospitals • Require high level of skills • Specialization helps reduce costs	**Aravind Eye Center.** A specialized network of eye hospitals in India providing the highest-quality eye care to low-income populations through efficient processes (chapter 8). **Narayana Hrudayalaya.** A network of specialized hospitals in India providing a variety of services at very low cost by using efficient processes (chapter 8).
Clinics • Require basic medically trained personnel (for example, nurses or community health workers) • Educate patients about common disease causes and treatments • Diagnose common ailments and prescribe basic treatments • Franchise models can increase visibility and help maintain quality	**One Family Health.** Franchised clinics in Rwanda operated by nurses providing basic health care diagnosis and treatment (chapter 6). **Janani.** A network of clinics in India providing family planning and basic health services to poor communities (chapter 6.)
Pharmacies • Require basic pharmaceutical personnel • Educate patients about treatment options • Franchise models can increase visibility and maintain supply chain, while reducing costs through bulk purchases	**Blue Star Bangladesh.** Franchised pharmacies providing treatment for common reproductive and child health issues (chapter 6).
Community Outreach • Requires only basic trained personnel • Educates consumers about common disease causes and treatments • Creates demand for services and products • Provides products at low cost	**Ethiopia Health Extension Worker Program.** A government program stationing health workers in rural villages to improve health awareness and provide basic services (chapter 6). **Living Goods.** Microentrepreneurs deployed to improve awareness among communities and sell basic health care products (chapter 6).

ly overcrowded and understaffed public hospitals in developing countries.

Much of the burden for hospitals in developing countries can be alleviated through more effective distribution systems for products and services, as described earlier. Hospitals must be integrated into the larger distribution system and able to refer patients to micropharmacies, microclinics, and entrepreneurs in patients' communities if they are to make effective use of their highly trained employees and limited space. As much as possible they must shift the burden of care to others to make the best use of their expensive facilities and skilled personnel. The integrated system we suggest offers many possibilities for such shifts. For example, patients can see clinicians, pharmacists, or even microentrepreneurs for most of their needs; only for the most complex and unusual cases do they need to visit a hospital. Making sure the poor have other available resources for receiving primary health care is an important step toward integrating hospitals into a comprehensive distribution system.

Specialized hospitals focus on a particular disease, condition, or ailment, and their factory like operations can drive down costs. They also use task shifting within their facilities to match the complexity of the task with the skill level of the employee.

The benefits of specialization have long been known, and specialization among health workers and hospitals has the same kinds of benefits. A specialized hospital can develop an expert staff through the increased number of procedures done per physician, and the fact that they can streamline their processes allows them to do far more procedures than can an average hospital. Economies of scale allow bulk purchasing, which reduces input costs.

Of course, specialization means such hospitals will need skilled laborers. And with specialization you need large numbers of patients to create economies of scale. They will therefore typically be found in urban areas.

To reduce costs, mid-level personnel instead of physicians can be used for basic tasks and telemedicine and/or traveling clinics can be used to reach rural communities. Efficient and effective services are particularly important where there is high demand.

Creating Demand

There is no shortage of simple, inexpensive solutions to solve health problems. Condoms can reduce unwanted pregnancy and the transmission of sexually transmitted infections, including HIV—and are cheap and easily distributed.[13] Maternal bleeding after childbirth—a major killer of mothers—can be prevented with the use of inexpensive and easy-to-use medication.[14] Breast milk is free, nutritious, and transfers immunity from the mother to her child.[15] Water can be purified with inexpensive and easy-to-use chlorine tablets.[16] Sleeping under a mosquito net greatly reduces the chances of getting malaria.[17] And exercise, a plant-based diet, smoking cessation, and even a daily aspirin can drastically reduce the chance of having a heart attack, stroke, and some cancers.[18] Although these solutions exist, it is critical to create demand for their use if they are to save lives.

Businesses are particularly skilled at creating demand, not only for their own product, but for their particular variety of the product—even when it is nearly identical to competitors' products. When people buy everything from aspirin to an automobile, most customers don't just grab the first that they find; they gravitate to a particular one. That 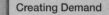 is generally because demand has been created for that product. We've been convinced that we not only need to have the product, but believe that one brand is superior to the others.

Businesses have much to teach about demand creation. And their lessons are not lost on those working to create global health impacts.

Creating demand for health care products and services can be accomplished through a variety of channels. Generating awareness and providing clear information on health issues and solutions can help to dispel long-held myths. Public awareness and

social marketing campaigns using mass media can improve awareness and knowledge within communities.[19]

Although these activities can take place on a regional, national,
or international level, studies indicate that interpersonal communication is most effective in creating change and catalyzing action.
We are most likely to listen to those we know or believe. For example, people will be more swayed by a message delivered by a
community health worker they know well and who lives in their
community than one delivered by a health worker who visits just
to deliver the health message. Likewise, these same community
members are more likely to be influenced by information delivered on a local radio station that specially targets that community
than by a national campaign.[20]

Regardless of the group or population size, there will generally be subgroups or subpopulations. Although the difference
between them may not be apparent to people outside the group,
to those on the inside the differences are clear and meaningful. As
a result, when we attempt to generate demand for a health care
project or service, particularly one where the benefit is not readily apparent, the differences between the subgroups can make a
tremendous difference, and we may need to approach each group
differently.

For example, for a variety of reasons the foreskin increases sus-
ceptibility to HIV transmission, and multiple studies have shown
that circumcision can reduce a man's risk for acquiring HIV by 60
percent.[21] It is a one-time procedure that can offer reduced risk
of acquiring HIV for the rest of the person's life. But creating
demand for this procedure, no matter how beneficial, would require particular creativity, as few—exceedingly few—men would
be willing to have their foreskin cut off without very persuasive
arguments delivered in the right way, by the right person, and at
a time they are receptive to both listening to and acting on the
information provided.

Consider Nyanza, one of eight provinces in Kenya and home
to the third-largest ethnic group in the country, the Luo. Nyanza is

a Bantu word for "large mass of water," for one of the things that makes the province distinctive is that it surrounds Lake Victoria. Unfortunately, it is distinctive in another way as well—the Luo men there have an HIV infection rate nearly twice the rate than the rest of the country.[22]

In Kenya, 80 percent of males are circumcised. However, circumcision rates vary highly across cultures and geographies. In Nyaza, 52 percent of the men from the Luo ethnic group were uncircumcised. These men also had the highest prevalence rate of HIV at nearly 15 percent.[23] As a result, the Ministry of Health launched a campaign to offer men voluntary circumcision. They initially engaged traditional leaders and mounted an awareness campaign to educate the community. They received large numbers of men who came in to be circumcised. However, as soon as the campaign ended, so too did high demand. After looking at their data, they realized that the campaign was effective in reaching young men, but not older men.[24] In subsequent campaigns, they have been able to reach new subpopulations by making slight changes in the message and outreach.

Demand creation cannot be static. It must be dynamic and changing—just as dynamic as the people they intend to reach and the communities in which they live. Given the subtle but important difference between subgroups and subpopulations and the need to get information out to communities, entrepreneurial community members are often effective at identifying the need and meeting it.

Increasingly NGOs and governments view these populations as customers, even when the product or service they are "selling" is lifesaving and at no cost to the customer. Unless NGOs or governments create demand for a product or service, additional supply will not be used. For example, in many countries over 40 percent of live births are attended by traditional birth attendants, even though traditional birth attendants may have little formal training and poor outcomes, and may even be banned from performing services by the government.[25] Many of these traditional birth attendants recognize that their customers have many options—other attendants, as well as NGO and government clinics, many of which are free—so like the entrepreneurs they are, they make their services accessible (in the home), acceptable, and affordable (for example, some may be willing to barter for payment).

Just as customers select options that may not work well, they too often ignore solutions that can save a life. For example, even though a simple salty-sweet solution composed of salt, sugar, water, and a zinc tablet costs only pennies and could prevent many of the 650,000 deaths due to diarrhea in children under five, it is often not used by many mothers in developing countries.[26] Entrepreneurs in developed countries, on the other hand, have created huge demand for a similar solution, but for a condition that is rarely life threatening—sweating caused by exercise. Sports drinks like Gatorade, Powerade, and many others are basically oral rehydration solutions—salty-sweet products used by many weekend athletes and others to help rehydrate. These sports drinks generate over $4 billion in annual revenue![27]

Most of these products condoms, chlorine tablets, bed nets, and aspirin—can be distributed right to those who need them using micropharmacies, health extension workers, or even a variety of microentrepreneurs, from door-to-door salespeople to a pharmacist on a bicycle. These methods can bring these easy solutions directly to the people and give entrepreneurs the opportunity to increase their income, improving both community health and wealth.

However, we need more than inexpensive and easy-to-deliver solutions—we need demand for a solution. Without demand, products and services won't be used, regardless of how inexpensive or readily available they are. People generally demand what they value. That means they must be educated on the value of various health products and services.

Champions

We all have people we admire, people we look up to, people whose opinions matter enough to us so we are willing to change our behaviors. It may be a friend, a teacher, a parent, a leader, or even a celebrity. These champions may be critical in helping to create demand for health products and services. Thus, it is important to have champions at local, regional, national, and international levels to create behavioral changes that will benefit people's health. These champions must be able to advocate for issues, marshal resources, and break through barriers. They must be able to influence policy and behavior in positive ways. And they must be able to give voice to the issues for those who are not heard and are most vulnerable, those who need interventions the most.

In engaging champions it is important to be clear and specific on the goals to achieve, to have messages coincide with pertinent and relevant events, and to use a variety of ways of getting the message out through a variety of champions. It is critically important that the issue be clearly defined for there to be impact. Champions will need to be provided with the data needed to support their arguments. And it is important for the organization to have a clear message if it is to have champions at many levels repeating that same message effectively.[28]

Champions should have:

- *Focus*—know the goal and target
- *Clarity*—be able to communicate the message clearly
- *Credibility*—be seen as a reliable source
- *Relevance*—be able to connect with people in ways that offer solutions to problems that are relevant to their lives
- *Good timing*—be able to articulate the message at a time when it can be linked to other critical issues and have the maximum impact
- *Commitment*—be dedicated to the issue and be willing to champion it over time [29]

These characteristics can be helpful in creating demand regardless of whether the focus is international or local, within one or multiple organizations.

Vouchers

Vouchers are like grocery store coupons: they can increase interest in a health product or service by reducing costs to the redeemer. The voucher can be used by patients to decide if, when, and where to get care. In addition, patient access to vouchers can increase competition among providers to give low-cost, quality care. Vouchers can create compelling incentives for patients to seek the care they need. While there have been debates about the relative merits of vouchers versus market-based strategies,[30] these approaches are influenced by local context and can complement each other.[31]

There are many compelling examples across the globe of effective implementations of vouchers. For example, in Tanzania they increased the use of insecticide-treated nets,[32] they have helped increase deliveries with birth attendants in Bangladesh,[33] and increased the use of sexually transmitted disease services for adolescents in Nicaragua.[34] In one voucher experiment in Uganda, mothers who were given vouchers to take motorcycle taxis to the clinic for prenatal care, delivery, and postnatal care were more likely to go to the clinic to receive these services. In the intervention, deliveries to clinics increased from 200 per month to 500 per month. In addition, more women came in for four or more prenatal visits.[35] In another study in Bangladesh, it was discovered that women with vouchers were 3.6 times more likely to have a skilled health person during delivery, 2.5 times more likely to deliver the baby in a health facility, 2.8 times more likely to receive postnatal care, twice as likely to get prenatal care, and 1.5 times more likely to seek treatment for obstetric complications.[36] Similar findings have been found in other voucher studies.[37]

The Need for Accountability

Accountability is essential. It demonstrates how actions and investment translate into tangible results and better long-term outcomes. Establishing clear goals and targets aligned with an organization's strategy supports effective decision-making. Regular 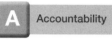 monitoring and evaluation let leaders identify when an organization's activities are not on track to meet targets, thereby cueing intervention. Evaluation efforts also help leaders determine the cost-effectiveness of program activities and when to reallocate limited resources.

Accountability measures are needed at all levels, from the international community down to individual microenterprises. At the international level, we have seen goal-making and tracking efforts take shape through the Millennium Development Goals. These eight goals, agreed upon by 189 countries in 2000, laid out specific and measurable targets with an explicit deadline of 2015. Through regular monitoring and publishing of reports, international leaders are able to identify when countries or regions are no longer on track to meet targets.[38]

Breaking the Bottleneck

Shifting tasks from a higher-level provider to a lower-level provider and from one setting to another may increase efficiency, reduce costs, and remove bottlenecks. Task shifting requires that lower-skilled providers be well trained and supported. Simplifying tasks, putting referral systems in place, and providing ongoing supervision can help task shifting be successful. Success in global health will also require maximizing efficiencies and effectiveness of interventions, and creating demand for them as well. Patients must be seen as customers, regardless of who covers the cost of services. Finally, goals, targets, and systems of accountability must be put in place so that we know where we're going and can tell when we get there. Accountability helps ensure that we measure what matters to achieve impacts in global health.

Food for Thought

- What safeguards might you put in place to ensure that you don't sacrifice quality for efficiency or vice versa?
- What three things can you do to help team members consistently meet targets for output, outcomes, and impacts?
- Which tasks now performed by highly skilled team members could be handed to others so you could have greater impact?

4

Tipping the Scales:
Scaling Up to Save Lives

Many exciting experiments and innovations in global health have the potential to dramatically improve the lives of millions in developing countries. These solutions do not need further scientific or technological refinement, but rather a business model that can disseminate these products and services to those in need in both urban and rural settings.

A critical part of the solution to creating impacts in global health is scaling up what works—getting the right solution to the right customer—all over the world.

Scaling Social Enterprises

There are poor-quality health programs that, when scaled, remained of low quality. Scaling bad programs may do more harm than good. And a number of health programs have achieved excellent quality outcomes in local-ized settings, but have generally  not been able to replicate and scale their successes to other settings.[1] What we need are high-quality global health products and services that can simultaneously achieve scale while maintaining high quality.

Quality at Scale: Is It Possible?

To scale quality programs in high-resource settings, we need leadership; effective collaboration with communities and governments; and monitoring, evaluation, and accountability.[2] But these prescriptions are insufficient for guiding scaling efforts in impoverished regions, where infrastructure is weak, resources are minimal, and education is not necessarily perceived as a right, or even a need. The obstacles are many, yet a handful of programs have successfully reached scale in these extremely challenging conditions.[3]

Some have distinguished different types of scaling.[4] Some scaling reflects geographic replication (for example, opening more distribution or treatment centers). Others reflect nonreplication options by affiliating with new partners or creating change in the environment, the community, or policy. Even with geographic replication, the challenges of moving to scale globally are significantly greater than opening another center a few miles away.

Previous scaling studies have focused largely on the strategic and organizational mechanisms and characteristics common to scaling efforts, both in developed-world contexts and in social enterprise more broadly. Among the factors important for scale are a theory of change;[5] organizational culture, structure, and leadership;[6] networks and affiliate interactions;[7] strategies for information sharing; and assessment of market readiness.[8] Others have argued that efforts to scale must be enhanced by activities that improve broader environmental features, such as regulations and infrastructure.[9]

A Model for Scaling Global Health

Our health model describes the factors most critical to bringing high-quality health programs to scale. This global health-scaling model can be used to develop high-quality, scalable programs that will be successful over long periods of time and across multiple geographic regions. It identifies the unique characteristics that enable some organizations to succeed where many private, NGO, and governmental programs are failing. Further relevant discussion of this model can be found in its application to education in developing countries.[10]

Scaling research has identified important scaling levers that can be helpful in scaling global health. These levers are 1) *programs* aligned to the clients' unique needs; 2) *processes* that enable programs to be offered at minimal cost; and 3) *passion* for organization goals and social impact (Table 6).[11]

Table 6 Levers for Scaling for Social Impact

Levers for Scaling	Key Features
Program	• Ensuring quality products, services, and delivery • Tailoring products and services to local contexts
Process	• Developing efficient processes to minimize costs • Providing appropriate training and support • Monitoring and evaluating activities
Passion	• Ensuring workforce commitment to organization goals • Empowering staff to make decisions and take risks • Adapting to changing environments

A number of organizations use all three of these levers. Though we have highlighted only one lever for each of the organizations discussed in the following sections, the organizations in fact make use of all three.

Program Scaling Levers

The first lever—program—refers to both the content and the delivery of the global health program. The role of this lever is to develop, conceptualize, and plan an initiative that meets the needs of the individuals as well as the larger community.

Available resources vary widely across regions, and programs must accommodate this fact. A strong program will consider local needs and experience. If a program is to be widely adopted, it must be tailored to the needs of individuals, families, and the

Idea in Action: Program Scaling Lever— CARE International

CARE International is an international nonprofit operating in over eighty countries and providing assistance to impoverished communities through programs in emergency relief, health, education, income generation, and advocacy. In 2011, because of its successful program scaling lever, CARE reached over 120 million people around the world through 1,100 projects.

The organization operates across the globe, implementing its program lever through its CARE members and host country offices. In each country where it operates CARE has a country office implementing all programs and projects. Each country office is run by a country coordinator and sets its own strategic plan. In addition to these country offices are twelve CARE members, independent nonprofits located in developed countries, including France, Japan, Australia, and the U.S. CARE members provide technical assistance, financing, human resources, and other types of support to projects in low-income countries.

By creating an organizational framework structured on the program scaling lever, CARE ensures that local communities actually desire its program activities. The country offices and country coordinator set the local strategic plan, which members must acknowledge and abide by. Since programs are implemented by the host country office, activities are culturally appropriate. Using this method, CARE provides tailored solutions for each context and encourages local community buy-in.[12]

broader community. If people do not sense the usefulness of the health products and services, we can expect little commitment on either the demand or supply side.[13] Taking sociocultural context into consideration will further ensure the highest quality of products, services, and delivery, and will require tailoring the program to specific needs.[14] Significant adaptation of successful programs is often necessary to achieve scale.

Process Scaling Levers

While the program levers focus on the quality characteristics of the program to be scaled, process levers focus on the mechanics of maintaining and replicating that quality at scale. In developing countries, efficiency in deploying and managing resources is essential; successful organizations build and manage their programs with scaling in mind. The need to maintain extremely low costs drives process engineering and standardization. The need for flexibility in diverse and changing conditions drives continuous monitoring and reconfiguration.[15]

Controlling costs is among the greatest challenges in achieving quality at scale.[17] Global health programs almost uniformly operate under significant resource constraints, but in the developing world funding constraints are typically severe.[18] Thus, organizations must consistently focus on maximizing the productivity of expenditures while eliminating activities that do not add value.

Efforts to systematize processes are sometimes perceived as "McDonaldizing" health. But although the primary objective is minimizing costs, such efforts also provide consistent, high-quality service delivery in challenging environments. As countries try to rapidly increase provision of quality global health services, for example, they often hit roadblocks such as lack of qualified health or administrative staff, or lack of adequate sites, resources, and materials for construction.[19] Obstacles such as these can often be overcome through the development of routines that accommodate the use of widely available human and material resources.[20]

While standardization of processes is essential for cost management, organizational actors should be empowered to tailor programs and activities to best meet the ongoing needs of clients and to improvise when circumstances make processes ineffective or impossible to execute properly.[21]

Ongoing health and administrative training provides the base level of support and capacity development essential for success. Training encourages professional development and aids in developing the necessary relationships among health workers and the

Ideas in Action: Process Scaling Lever—World Vision

The Midwife Mobile Phone Project, created by World Vision International, a faith-based organization started in 1950 that works with local communities to improve health, education, and economic development across the globe, is a good example of the process scaling lever at work.

The Midwife Mobile Phone Project is a program created in Indonesia after the 2004 tsunami left much of the region with limited access to health care. The program was created to deal with the displacement or death of a large number of midwives due to the tsunami. By using mobile communications the project aimed to facilitate, accelerate, and improve the efficiency and quality of services. The program provided mobile phones for a new cohort of midwives and developed a health information database that allowed health workers to upload patient health information via SMS (Short Message Service) text messaging.

The mobile phones allowed efficient communication between midwives and patients. They also improved communication between midwives and doctors, so that midwives could attain more medical knowledge. Above all, the mobile phones created a more efficient environment for midwives. Instead of having to repeatedly travel to patients' homes to monitor their status, midwives could use SMS to identify when their presence was actually needed.

World Vision's use of mobile phones is an example of a program incorporating the process lever to improve impact. The mobile phones allowed midwives to efficiently use their limited time and resources. The mobile phones also provided a channel of support for midwives by directly connecting them with highly trained doctors. The development of a centralized database that allowed midwives to upload patient data via SMS created an efficient method of monitoring the program and health outcomes.[16]

various NGO, government, and business leaders pivotal to ensuring sustainable success in scaling.[22] Once effective processes and support mechanisms have been established, ongoing oversight is needed to ensure that programs are scaling effectively and program delivery and quality standards are maintained.[23] Continuous monitoring and evaluation provide the transparency necessary to drive accountability for actions and results.

A clear logic model lays out the relationships among investments, actions, and ultimate outcomes and provides a framework for accountability and achieving goals such as improved health, poverty reduction, and quality of life. As a result, each organization should also be engaged in monitoring and evaluation at a variety of stages, including resources obtained and employed, activities conducted, services delivered, direct program outcomes, and social impact.

The systems of accountability rely both on diagnostic metrics and interactive discussions about the knowledge to be gleaned from the measures and ways to best redesign programs and processes. These systems productively channel information toward continual program improvement.[24]

Passion Scaling Levers

Passion provides the motivation and energy to move from plans and ideas to successful health programs. Simultaneous achievement of excellence and scale under challenging developing-country conditions requires an entire range of dedicated stakeholders with a strong belief in the organization and its mission.[25]

Engagement is a core element of passion and motivates stakeholders to achieve success despite the constraints and other barriers faced by new global health programs. Most global health organizations have ongoing funding and staffing challenges. Yet all key organizational participants need to be highly engaged with their organizations and projects. Both volunteers and paid staff must be strongly committed to both their organizations and to the clients served, since working in developing-world health typically involves harsh working conditions along with a variety of risks and uncertainties.

Employees in successful organizations such as BRAC tend to operate with a sense of ownership of the organization and its programs, a factor that increases their passion to help the program succeed. Employees are empowered to pursue opportunities and are provided with the freedom to take risks and to directly discuss issues with key organizational decision makers. Empowerment is an important aspect of program ownership, which is essential in programs operating at scale.[26]

In developing countries roads flood, electricity goes out, health funding is pulled, contracts are violated, and idealized plans become impossible to execute. Employees need the power and organizational support to rapidly and flexibly address new challenges, and the organization must be able to learn from these solutions and reconfigure operations to accommodate them in the future. To address the needs of ever-changing circumstances, organizations must foster collaborative and open environments that enable exchange of ideas and sharing of concerns.[27]

Prior work on social enterprise scaling has emphasized higher-level scaling levers, such as staffing, communication, alliance building, lobbying, earnings-generation replication, and stimulation of market forces.[29] Our approach looks at a more fundamental core of scaling drivers. Quality programs, effective processes, and even passion are treated as givens by most current scaling literature. But the very poor quality of many large global health systems, the high resource requirements of most high-quality systems, and the lack of a push toward growth and impact suggests that these more fundamental levers cannot be overlooked.

Moving to Scale

Scaling global health programs for the poor remains a significant challenge, yet the need for high-quality, low-cost health is enormous. Only a handful of organizations have been able to scale programs effectively. Our model describes the most successful or-

Ideas in Action: Passion Scaling Lever—BRAC

BRAC, formerly Bangladesh Rural Advancement Committee, is the world's largest NGO, reaching an estimated 126 million people around the globe as of December 2011. Initially starting in Bangladesh, BRAC now operates in more than ten countries around the world providing a wide range of services for poor communities, including economic development, health, and education. Much of its success can be traced to its use of the passion lever.

BRAC's Essential Health Care (EHC) program provides community-level services and solutions focusing on nutrition education, clean water, family planning, maternal health, and other basic health needs. Although BRAC employs paid health workers, its program is highly dependent on the passion of its nearly 100,000 health volunteers. These volunteers are located in local communities and provide door-to-door services to tackle the ten most common diseases, including anemia and diarrhea. The female volunteers are participants in BRAC's microfinance programs and are local community members.

BRAC is an example of an organization effectively implementing the passion lever, in this case by leveraging its microfinance program to recruit EHC workers and volunteers. Since the women come from the communities they serve, they have an investment in the success of the program. Without the commitment of these women and their willingness to volunteer, BRAC would not be able to reach the scale and impact it has achieved.[28]

ganizations in an effort to articulate the factors these organizations considered most essential in their success. These three levers are essential and include a high-quality program suited to the health needs of the individual and community, efficient processes and effective systems for supporting and overseeing those processes, and passionate engagement at all levels supported by distributed authority to adjust to changing needs.

Developing a program that clients in those environments will embrace requires marketing that can integrate significant local knowledge and a deep understanding of the lives of the clients. This requires programs of extremely high quality that have been developed by experts to meet the unique needs of individuals and communities in need.[30] It also requires overcoming the many barriers to achieving scale:

- Shortage of financial resources
- Shortage of human resources in health
- Shortage of human resources in enterprise management
- Lack of infrastructure—roads, hospitals, electricity, water, and other factors
- Lack of education
- Lack of coordinated government, NGO, and for-profit activities
- Lack of innovative, entrepreneurial, and skilled leadership in government, NGO, and for-profit enterprises
- Lack of focus on mission and priorities

Designing processes that can operate effectively under extreme resource constraints also requires special attention and effort. Despite constraints, government leaders and communities expect health programs to deliver high-quality products and services. Thus, they need to recognize the importance of service quality and develop scripted processes that make possible high levels of consistency with expected outcomes and enhanced by frameworks enabling communication and support among health workers.

Finally, developing and maintaining the passion needed to work with these difficult-to-serve populations, and to overcome the continuous variety of problems and risks that arise, requires an organization that can find and support devoted and engaged participants. This includes recognizing the importance of regularly engaging with staff to maintain high levels of passion for the organization and its mission while operating in extremely challenging circumstances. Extensive communication is essential.

By focusing heavily on the fundamentals of program, process, and passion, organizations operating in even the most challenging conditions can achieve scale while maintaining outstanding quality. Researchers and practitioners seeking to develop scaling models to meet market challenges can benefit by using these fundamental organizational levers to deliver high-quality health care to everyone who needs it.[31]

Partnership Coordination

Achieving scale in global health requires partners. No one entity can or should try to address all health issues alone. A variety of partnerships can be created between entities and sectors: between private businesses, between governments, and between government and private 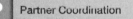 businesses. We will focus on public-private partnerships and franchising because of their ability to create more effective means of achieving desired impacts.

Public-Private Partnerships

Public-private partnerships allow governments, NGOs, and businesses to collaborate and work in ways no single organization or sector could do alone. Though sometimes complicated to successfully implement, partnerships create potential win-win opportunities to build sustainable markets for health products and services that would be difficult to create without coordination. These strategies often lead to bold actions that can lead to dramatic improvements in reducing illness and death.[32]

Public-private partnerships can be created for a variety of causes, including product development, improved access to care, advocacy and education, regulation and quality assurance, and strengthened health services. There are significant benefits to such partnerships, including the infusion of private capital; the management and increased efficiency found in private companies; the creation of cost-effective, high-quality goods and services for target populations; and the ability to overcome challenges that arise when any single actor attempts to tackle global health issues.[33]

Despite the potential benefits, partnerships can be difficult to maintain, especially when goals and values fail to align. There must be evaluation methods to measure outcomes and a strong legislative and governance framework to deal with multiple parties, since there is a real possibility of conflicts when trying to combine the priorities and values of for-profit companies, NGOs, and governments. Initial coordination and ongoing monitoring and evaluation can be problematic when one is dealing with different organizations with different goals and values. This can have a negative effect on the long-term sustainability of health care systems in poor countries. But with clear communication and a clear agreed-upon mission and purpose among all parties involved, many of these issues can be overcome.

The GAVI Alliance (formerly the Global Alliance for Vaccines and Immunisation) is one example of successful management innovation through a public-private partnership. The GAVI Alliance is a partnership among the key drivers of immunization in the world, including organizations involved in immunization strategy and policy setting, advocacy, fundraising, vaccine development and procurement, and in-country support and immunization delivery. The alliance helps each country stimulate demand for immunizations and create mechanisms for service delivery. It also negotiates prices with pharmaceutical companies and, once a price is set, supports countries in buying vaccines.

The GAVI partnership thus creates a win for the countries, which are able to purchase vaccines at deep discounts; a win for the pharmaceutical companies, which now have guaranteed and stable sales; and a win for children, who receive lifesaving vaccines. Since 2000, GAVI estimates that this partnership has enabled it to save 5.5 million lives through vaccination of children in developing countries (see chapter 5 for details on GAVI).[34]

Of course, public-private partnerships are not the only kinds of partnerships. There can be any number of partnerships between entities operating in the global health arena. Many, if not most, require the creation of multidisciplinary teams, where people with different kinds of expertise can come together and to create better health outcomes for a given population. The varieties are endless. At the upper level, uReport, a crowd-sourcing solution using SMS, was developed by a combination of government, university, and NGOs, in Uganda and elsewhere, and a private telecom company. Partnerships do not have to be international conglomerations—they can simply include two local entrepreneurs who work together to improve effectiveness and efficiency and increase profits. One could, for example, create a partnership by placing a micro-pharmacy next to a clinic. The result will be, in each case, to increase scale. To make each of these collaborations work requires entrepreneurship on the part of those seeking to create them.

Partnerships through Franchising

Franchises are another kind of partnership, typically pairing entrepreneurs with NGOs or for-profit businesses. Through franchising, microentrepreneurs can access some of the advantages of big businesses, including economies of scale and training. The franchisee runs its business on a profit/loss basis, so it has a strong incentive to provide good products and services at an affordable cost. One of the roles of the franchisor is to provide a common brand to assure quality while using its buying power to reduce the overall cost of inputs and supplies to franchisees. In addition, the franchisee receives support from the central organization and benefits from brand recognition.

Meanwhile, franchising benefits the central organization because it is able to reach more places more easily without attempting to exercise the kind of central control that can result in bad decisions being made by people far away from where the problems arise. As a result, franchising allows organizations to scale up their operations rapidly and efficiently. Franchising also provides entrepreneurial opportunities for community members, helping the organization gain credibility by putting a local face behind each of the branches.[35]

To work, a franchise organization needs to have a successful and proven initial management concept, sufficient demand for the product or service, a strong supply chain to ensure that goods are delivered regularly so that stocks do not become depleted, and a well-respected brand. The network model needs to be extremely simple, and the organization needs to focus on well-documented successes. Location is important as well. Franchisees should be close to customers, but spread out enough to ensure that there is enough demand per store.[36]

There are also several challenges to attracting and retaining franchisees. The franchisees may need access to financing for the initial startup costs—and one can expect that franchisees will have to compete for financing opportunities. Local political and regulatory environments matter a great deal—the same operation might be legal in one place but illegal in another. To maintain the brand's value, the organization has to maintain quality control, since any negative reputation for the brand will impact all franchisees, and this is only complicated by the need to manage and interact with a large number of geographically dispersed franchisees.[37]

Many of these problems can be solved by having a comprehensive and ongoing set of training programs, as well as regular meetings at all levels. There should be a feedback system for franchisee input into decision-making. Providing effective advertising and strong brand recognition will help keep franchisees operational by creating demand. Finally, help services and financial and managerial reports can be offered to assist franchisees in improving their businesses. By doing these things, an organization should be able to set up a successful franchise operation—one that can get health goods and services to the people who need them, when they need them, and where they need them.[38]

The solutions highlighted above involve the creation of franchises, which is one way of creating a hierarchical network in a hub–spoke model, with a central organization able to send smaller and smaller fingers out into more and more rural areas. This model works because franchise models are able to take advantage of economies of scale. A benefit of locating a business or organization in urban areas is that one can achieve economies of scale—the larger you get, the cheaper it becomes to make your product or provide your service.

However, most of the people we need to reach in places like Africa and Asia are rural. The franchise model allows us to both create economies of scale and reach rural areas. We can see this in the fact that it is impossible to drive through even the most rural areas of the United States without eventually running into a Shell gas station, a 7-Eleven, or a McDonald's. For rural people in particular, hospitals and large clinics and pharmacies are not realistic options. Microclinics, micropharmacies, and even people on motorcycles or bicycles have to fill the gap. By franchising to local entrepreneurs who understand the local population, large companies are able to reach more people in more places, while the entrepreneurs are able to take advantage of the fact that they are offering a well-known brand.[39]

Pros and Cons of Franchising

Pros	Cons
• Standardization	• Limited flexibility
• Use of a proven business model	• Franchise fees
• Collective purchasing power	• Vulnerability to negative franchise reputation
• Economies of scale	
• Common branding	

Scaling What Works

To succeed, we need to harness all of the *IMPACTS* elements to deliver health care goods and services. Given the effective health products and services at our disposal, the real problem—and the main focus of this book—is how to get these solutions to those who need them.

To have significant impact in global health, we need to scale up what works. Scaling requires a focus on ensuring that the critical elements of the program are present, efficient processes to ensure quality are in place, and an empowered workforce can adapt a program to local contexts. Furthermore, partnerships must be created within and between sectors. No one party is capable of tackling global health alone. Partnerships allow for a sharing of strengths and can create a sum that is greater than individual parts. In order to achieve the most strides in global health, we must look for strategic partners to collaborate with.

In Part 2, we will show how some organizations in developing countries are working to create impacts in health. These organizations exemplify many or all of the *IMPACTS* elements, and we will see a wide variety of providers and organizations, small microentrepreneurs, governments, NGOs, and multinational corporations all working together to benefit the lives of others.

Food for Thought

- How can you best maintain quality as you expand?
- What five things might be limiting demand for your products or services? What might you do to overcome these obstacles within the next year?

Part 2
IMPACTS in Motion

5

The Warmth of a Mother's Touch:
Maternal and Child Health

Sadiki lay in pain, exhausted, on the floor of her home in Malindi, a rural village in Kenya. She had been in labor for more than twenty hours. She wondered why this birth was so much more difficult than her previous one. Maybe it was because her husband had been by her side back then. But after a roadside accident made her a widow at twenty-four with a set of twins at home and a baby on the way, all of life seemed different.

After her husband's death, Sadiki received aid from the Caris Family Foundation, an international NGO focused on helping single mothers develop health and business skills. Entrepreneurial by nature and now even more motivated, she began mastering skills and dreamed of opening a small daycare center after the baby was born.

But for now, her only desire was to end the pain.

This baby seemed way too big. So much bigger, she thought, than her twins—combined. Maybe she shouldn't have listened to the community health worker's suggestion to get prenatal care. Maybe the supplements they'd given her and the healthier food she was eating had made the baby too big for her small body to handle.

The community health workers had urged her to call a *tuk-tuk*, a three-wheeled motorized taxi, to go to the hospital as soon as the labor pains set in. But she had ignored them, and, like most of the women in her village, she summoned the traditional birth attendant when her time came and prepared to give birth at home.

Knowing the baby was soon due, the community health workers stopped by to check on Sadiki. That's when they found her on the ground, nearly unconscious. Over the objection of the traditional birth attendant, they loaded Sadiki's limp body into the waiting vehicle and, as they were trained, rushed her to the hospital. As soon as she arrived, she was whisked away for an emergency C-section. She delivered another set of twins, a boy and a girl. But this time only one survived.

She named her Amani—Swahili for *peace*, Arabic for *aspiration*.

Worldwide, every two minutes a woman dies of pregnancy or delivery complications; every six seconds a baby less than a year old dies.[1] In nearly every case they are living in a country like Kenya, in a village like Malindi, and in a home like Sadiki's.

Despite the recent progress made in reducing maternal mortality, we still lose over 250,000 mothers annually due to pregnancy-related causes—an unacceptably high statistic by any measure.[2] A mother makes sure that her children have clothing, food, a safe place to sleep, an education, and care when they are sick.[3] She is the sole provider in one-third of the world's households, and if she dies her children are up to ten times more likely to die as well.[4] But that's not all. Women provide 60 to 80 percent of agricultural labor in developing countries, producing half the world's food.[5] At home, they prepare food, collect water, and care for the children, sick, and elderly. When women are lost, entire communities suffer.

Over the past two decades, maternal and child deaths have been reduced by 30 percent and child deaths by 40 percent.[6] However, for these deaths to continue to fall, successful interventions need to be dramatically scaled up to reach the millions who currently don't have access to even basic maternal and child health care.

By using proven technological and business model innovations and entrepreneurial solutions we can save millions of moms and babies.

The Critical Periods to Save Mothers and Babies

To save pregnant women and their children, simple and innovative solutions can improve the access, use, quality, and cost of care during three critical periods for moms and babies: family planning, pregnancy and delivery, and early childhood.

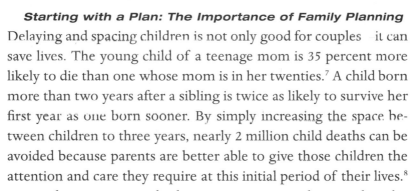

Family Planning → *Pregnancy & Delivery* → *Early Childhood*

Starting with a Plan: The Importance of Family Planning

Delaying and spacing children is not only good for couples   it can save lives. The young child of a teenage mom is 35 percent more likely to die than one whose mom is in her twenties.[7] A child born more than two years after a sibling is twice as likely to survive her first year as one born sooner. By simply increasing the space between children to three years, nearly 2 million child deaths can be avoided because parents are better able to give those children the attention and care they require at this initial period of their lives.[8]

For these reasons and others, it is important that couples who wish to delay childbirth have access to effective means of birth control. The most effective reversible contraceptives are medical, such as implants and intrauterine devices that can be inserted by trained community health workers and last three to five years. When a woman decides to have a child, the devices can be reversed (Table 7).[9]

Even though contraceptive use has increased sixfold over the past fifty years in developing countries, more than three-quarters of women of childbearing age who wish to avoid pregnancy in Sub-Saharan Africa do not have easily available access to contraceptives, nor do the majority of women in South Asia.[10]

Access to effective contraceptives could reduce both unwanted pregnancies and many of the 44 million abortions worldwide that result from them each year.[11]

Table 7 Comparison of Contraceptive Methods

Contraceptive Method[a]	Percent Annual Chance of Unintended Pregnancy	Requirements
Contraceptive implants[b]	0.05%	One-time implant (three-year lifespan)
Sterilization	0.15–0.5%	One-time surgery
Intrauterine devices	0.2–0.8%*	One-time implant (five-year lifespan)
Hormone injections (such as Depo-Provera)	6%	Quarterly follow-up
Birth control pill	9%	Monthly checkup
Diaphragm	12%	
Male condom	18%	Community education
Withdrawal	22%	Community education
Fertility awareness	24%	Community education
None	85%	

[a] As typically done.
[b] These are small rods implanted under the skin that slowly release contraceptive hormones such as Implanon.
Source: Trussell (2011) *Contraceptive Efficacy*.

Family Planning — Pregnancy & Delivery — Early Childhood

Staying Alive While Giving Birth

Too often, while giving birth to new life, a woman loses her own. The vast majority of these women die from preventable causes, such as severe bleeding, infections, unsafeabortions, and hypertensive crises.[12] Pregnancy and childbirth is particularly risky for younger teenage girls. A mother under fifteen is five times more likely to die during childbirth than one in her twenties.[13]

While it is best for both mothers and babies for deliveries to occur in equipped medical facilities with skilled personnel, that may not be possible for many women who live in remote regions, or who have other significant barriers to care. Fortunately, midwives and traditional birth attendants can be trained to use appropriate medications to decrease maternal bleeding, and to reduce the risk of infection for the mother and newborn during labor and delivery.[14]

Every Child Deserves a Fifth Birthday

We can save many of the 7 million children under age five we lose each year from preventable diseases. More than 30 percent of these children die within their first month of life. At least half of these deaths can be prevented with means that we already have available.[15] Moreover, for every newborn who dies, twenty more suffer from birth-related injuries or complications that cause learning difficulties or other health conditions—many of which are permanent.[16] Many of these poor outcomes for children could be prevented by providing solutions such as clean water, vaccinations, breastfeeding during infancy, and mosquito nets to sleep under.[17]

Clean Water. Diarrheal disease is a leading cause of death in children, taking 650,000 lives a year.[18] It is both preventable and treatable. Children who drink contaminated water often get diarrhea and become very dehydrated. Their small bodies are unable to handle the rapid shift in body fluids. Oral rehydration solution (ORS), a simple homemade concoction of water, sugar, and salt, with a zinc tablet, can in most cases prevent dehydration. This simple treatment has saved 50 million children in the past twenty-five years, and could easily save many millions more if it was distributed to and used by those in need.[19]

However, the best solution to prevent diarrhea, and host of other diseases is by giving children clean water. There are a number of inexpensive and innovative ways to clean contaminated water. Chlorine tablets are a cheap and effective solution for cleaning dirty water, costing just pennies and taking minutes to use. Filters are an alternative to using chlorine. LifeStraw, a filter made by Vestergaard Frandsen, filters water instantly through a strawlike device and lasts up to five years. Its production is subsidized by carbon credits the company receives as its use reduces emissions that would come from burning fuel to boil water.[20]

Tata Chemicals has developed an innovative, low-cost water filter system that uses rice husks, a common waste product in India, to filter water at very low cost.[21] On a larger scale, GE's Sunspring, a solar-powered water plant used in the Haiti earthquake relief effort, can process 5,000 gallons per day for up to ten years. This allows even the most remote areas in developing nations to get clean water.[22]

The Coca-Cola Company has a number of projects to provide clean water in developing countries. However, to scale up these efforts in more sustainable ways, it recently teamed up with innovator and entrepreneur Dean Kamen and his DEKA Research and Development Corporation. DEKA has designed Slingshot, a water purification device that produces clean, drinkable water from contaminated water. The device boils and evaporates water from rivers, oceans, and other dirty sources and collects clean water once the vapor has condensed. Each unit is capable of producing 10 gallons of clean water an hour, enough to serve 300 people. Designed to run on less electricity than a hair dryer, the Slingshot device can be powered by a generator, solar cells, or biomass.

Though the technology has promise, it is cost prohibitive for developing countries when produced in small quantities. This is a technology feasible only at scale. To dramatically reduce costs, DEKA aims to increase volume and exploit economies of scale. DEKA's partnership with the Coca-Cola Company plans to test the implementation of the prototypes and then rapidly scale up production. The partnership aims to deliver Slingshot devices to schools, clinics, and community centers throughout the world and provide millions of gallons of clean drinking water to rural communities.[23]

Vaccines. After birth, children can be saved by vaccines and clean water. Vaccinations are one of the most cost-effective solutions in preventing childhood deaths. GAVI and other childhood immunization efforts have helped scale up immunization programs, which prevent an estimated 2.5 million child deaths a year.[24] Unfortunately, many children still do not receive these life-saving solutions. An additional 2 million deaths among children under age five could be prevented if currently available vaccines were more widely distributed.[25] Vaccines not only reduce the number of childhood deaths, they also prevent major illnesses and long-term disability.

The GAVI Alliance is a public private partnership launched in 2000 to increase access to lifesaving vaccines in low-income countries. The partnership was formed by donor countries, developing countries, international aid organizations, and the vaccine industry, and includes the World Bank, WHO, UNICEF, the Bill and Melinda Gates Foundation, and many others. GAVI requires host countries to initiate participation and contribute financial resources, ensuring that vaccination efforts are incorporated within the nation's larger health care strategy.

The partnership has created innovative finance structures that give the pharmaceutical industry incentives to invest in research and development on diseases primarily impacting low-income countries. In addition, host countries are supported by GAVI's guidance on program design, mobilization, and monitoring. The partnership has been extremely successful in increasing access to vaccines. Coverage of basic immunization has reached nearly 80 percent in GAVI-supported countries.[26] Through GAVI-supported vaccination programs, an estimated 5.5 million deaths from hepatitis B, measles, influenza, and other diseases have been averted.[27]

Developments in technology are making vaccines easier to deliver and distribute. Delivery systems are transitioning from needle-based delivery to easier methods, such as skin patches, oral drops, and aerosol sprays. In addition, heat-stable vaccines can reduce the cost of distribution by removing the need for refrigerated transportation.[28] As some of these technologies become more available and effectively distributed, even more lives can be saved.

Saving Mothers and Babies: The Basics

Saving the lives of mothers and their babies is not complicated in most cases. Prenatal care can help ensure that problems are prevented or anticipated, and that when they occur providers are available and equipped to help. Most of what is needed is basic education, supplies, and care for common issues and access to more advanced clinical care when complications arise (Table 8).[29]

- *Basic Knowledge.* Basic knowledge involves learning how to avoid unplanned pregnancies, the benefits of prenatal care, and the importance of delivery within an equipped facility with a skilled attendant. It also involves learning why it is important for children to be breast-fed, vaccinated, and sleep under mosquito nets. Mothers must learn how to make sure that they and their families use only clean water.
- *Basic Supplies.* The supplies needed are also basic, such as contraceptives, chlorine or other methods to purify water, routine antibiotics, oral rehydration solution to prevent deaths from dehydration during diarrhea, and insecticide-treated mosquito nets.
- *Basic Care.* Most of care, diagnosis, and treatment of un-complicated cases of pneumonia, diarrhea, and malaria can be provided in community settings, small clinics, or people's homes. About 15 percent of all births have complications that could be fatal if not diagnosed and treated promptly.[30] Optimally, women should deliver in equipped facilities under the supervision of skilled birth attendants. However, when

Table 8 Solutions to Prevent Most Maternal and Infant Deaths

Problem	Annual Impact Worldwide	Solution	Trained Provider
Unplanned pregnancy	86 million unplanned births; 41 million abortions	Contraception	Community health worker
Maternal deaths	255,000 women	Prenatal care Skilled attendant Birthing center	Nurse or midwife
Neonate* deaths	>2.24 million newborns	Prenatal care Skilled attendant Birthing center	Nurse or midwife
Pneumonia	846,000 children	Early diagnosis Antibiotics Vaccination Breastfeeding	Community health worker
Diarrhea	665,000 children	Clean water Oral rehydration solution Vaccination	Community health worker
Malaria	1.17 million people (56% children under age 5)	Mosquito nets Antimalarials	Community health worker
Malnutrition	Related to 35% of all child deaths	Breastfeeding Micronutrients	Community health worker

* The neonatal period is from birth to one year of age.
Sources: Singh, Sedgh, and Hussain (2010) "Unintended Pregnancy: Worldwide Levels, Trends, and Outcomes"; Lozano et al. (2012) "Global and Regional Mortality from 235 Causes of Death for 20 Age Groups in 1990 and 2010"; World Health Organization (2012) "Children: Reducing Mortality Fact Sheet."
Note: Lozano et al. estimate 2010 malaria deaths as 1.17 million, a 20% increase from 1990. This data differs from the 2012 World Malaria Report, which, using different methodology, reports 660,000 malaria deaths for 2010.

such a facility is not available, health workers can be trained to deliver in the home or other community setting. The most common cause of maternal death is post-partum hemorrhage, and community-based health workers, including traditional birth attendants, can be trained to safely administer medications to reduce risk of post-partum hemorrhage when women are unable to deliver in equipped facilities.[31]

There are many examples in both the public and private sectors of excellent care being provided for mothers and children right in the community by trained and supervised community health workers and volunteers who are linked to more experienced providers and equipped facilities.

Public Options That Work

Ethiopia: Bringing Effective Contraceptives to the Women Who Need Them

Ethiopia is the second-largest country in Africa, with a population of 84 million. In 2000, it was one of the world's most underdeveloped countries, ranking number 171 out of 174 countries in the Human Development Index, a measurement of health, education, and income.[32] As in most Sub-Saharan African countries at the time, only 8 percent of Ethiopia's married women were using contraception.[33] The low rates of contraceptive use were related to the fact that 82 percent of Ethiopians lived in rural regions; nearly 60 percent lived more than six miles from the nearest health facility, and most did not have easy access to transportation.[34]

By 2005, use of contraceptives had increased to 15 percent, still very low given that nearly half of married Ethiopians wished to delay or stop childbearing.[35] Of the women fortunate enough to obtain contraceptives, two-thirds received injectables, requiring them to return to the health clinic every three months for additional injections. Due to poor distribution channels, these injectable contraceptives were frequently out of stock when women arrived.[36]

To combat this problem Ethiopia began task-shifting contraceptive implants from the hospital and clinics to health extension workers (HEWs) who are based in communities throughout the country and are linked to health 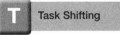 facilities. The Ethiopian Health Extension Program was designed to increase primary health care access in the community. Since 2004, the Ministry of Health has trained 35,000 workers and coordinates and monitors the program. Health extension workers are based primarily in rural regions and deliver a standard package of seventeen health care messages, including education about disease prevention and control (for example, HIV/AIDS, STIs, and TB), first aid, family planning, basic maternal and child health care, immunization, nutrition, hygiene, and environmental health. They also distribute immunizations and injectable contraceptives and can treat dysentery, intestinal parasites, and other ailments. They refer complicated cases to the nearest health center when necessary. By 2010, maternal deaths in Ethiopia had dropped by 50 percent and child deaths by 26 percent over a ten-year period (Table 9).[37]

Rwanda: The Little Country That Could

One of the more impressive success stories in health improvement in a low-income country is Rwanda. This small landlocked country of 11.37 million was devastated by genocide in 1994 that left 800,000 people dead, affecting everyone in the country.[38] The tragedy occurred over a month, leaving hundreds of thousands of orphans, broken families, raped women infected with HIV, and maimed and injured people. All of this happened in a country already struggling with high rates of disease, illiteracy, and other social problems.

However, as we noted in the introduction, when our backs are against the wall, we become innovative and entrepreneurial. Rwanda did just that. In 2000, Rwanda had a maternal mortality rate of 1,071 per 100,000 live births—almost 20 percent higher than in Africa as a whole. And Africa had the worst maternal mortality rate in the world—more than double the world average. Child mortality was no better. In 2000, on the worst continent for health, Rwanda was near the bottom.[39]

But what a difference a decade makes! By 2010, maternal mortality had been cut by 60 percent, and child deaths had dropped by the same percentage.[40]

So what did Rwanda do?

To combat its high rates of maternal and child deaths, Rwanda in 2000 began improving its health facilities and began task-shifting basic services to the community through an exciting all-volunteer CHW program, Animateurs de Santé (Table 9). In the program, each community selects three CHWs, including one who focuses on pregnant women and children under a year old. Because the CHWs are selected by the community, they are also responsible to the community.

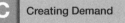

Community Health Workers monitor child milestone attainment and distribute family planning supplies, including condoms, contraceptive pills, and injectable contraceptives. They are able to give antibiotics for some illnesses, but for the most part they refer patients to nearby clinics for care. For pregnant women, the CHWs ensure that women attend prenatal visits, sleep under insecticide-treated bed nets to prevent malaria, deliver their babies in a health facility, and receive and understand information on proper nutrition, contraception, pregnancy, HIV, and malaria.[41]

Rwanda had a clear target to achieve. However, by 2006, despite the potential of the CHW program, death rates were not dropping fast enough for the government to achieve its target.[42] In response, it implemented both demand (directed toward mothers and valued at $10) and supply-side (directed toward the CHWs) non-cash incentives for pregnancy, delivery, and postnatal care. Within the first nine months of this program, 86 percent more women accessed prenatal services, and 16 percent more women delivered in the hospital![43]

Complementing the CHW program to stimulate demand and supply is Rwanda's health insurance program, which started around the same time. Consumers can select their plan, ranging from a very basic plan to one that covers all services and drugs provided by the health center as well as ambulance transport to a district hospital. Premiums and copayments do vary based on income. The average premium is $1.80 per family member; the very poor, approximately 20 percent of the population, pay nothing.[44]

The health insurance scheme has also created incentives for the private sector to increase the supply of health services. Child and Family Wellness (CFW), a maternal and child health franchise that originated in Kenya, began operating in Rwanda partly in response to the incentives that the negotiated health insurance brings.

To promote high-quality care, the government of Rwanda implemented a pay-for-performance scheme as a financial incentive for government-sponsored health care facilities. The scheme pays bonuses to primary health care centers based on fourteen maternal and child health indicators, including the reason for patient visits and the type of services delivered. These performance indicators are then paired with facility quality factors to determine the payment bonus rewarded.[45]

A World Bank study showed that the incentive program was associated with an increase in the quality and number of maternal and child health services provided. In fact, providers began encouraging women to deliver in facilities because of the associated financial rewards. Some even had health workers conduct community outreach to find pregnant women to deliver at the health facilities.[46]

Many other government-sponsored community health programs have been similarly successful (see the summary in Table 9). Many of these programs provide a salary to the workers (for example, Ethiopia, Malawi, Brazil, and Pakistan), while others provide nonfinancial incentives, such as recognizing the CHW as a community leader. Ongoing training and supervision of these CHWs, as well as linking them to backup support for more advanced needs, is critical for task shifting to work well in these programs.

Private Options That Work

Public options for community-based care for mothers and children can work well when the government is stable; there is a well-functioning health infrastructure; community providers are trained, supervised, and linked to the health system; and effective quality control mechanisms are in place. Unfortunately, many countries fall short in some or many of these areas. Even where the public health system is strong, government cannot meet the challenges alone. Therefore, it is essential that there be private options as well, since they can play a critical role in supporting public options to ensure that women and children get the care that they need.

Private Option Varieties: Basic Care

There are a number of private options to improve health care for women and children in developing countries. In many cases these options have developed out of necessity: women and children were dying. Even stable governments in developing countries face herculean challenges providing just basic and essential services— sanitation, education, electricity, food, water, security—so health care often takes a back seat. In places that are unstable or plagued with corruption, services may be crumbling.

If you go to any developing country, you are likely to find a host of chemists, pharmacists, and health practitioners operating out of their homes and small shops. They are often micro-entrepreneur practitioners, and they are generally unregulated, unlicensed, and do not have much formal training. The most commonly used options used by women and children include traditional birth attendants, and franchised or networked private health enterprises.

Traditional Birth Attendants. Traditional birth attendants (TBAs) provide the majority of maternal and early childhood care in many low-income countries and some middle-income countries as well, particularly for the poor. They are often seasoned or older women who have had children themselves and serve to

Table 9 Task-Shifting Government Health Services for Women and Children

Country	Features	Progress (2000–2010)
Brazil	• 246,000 trained workers, each responsible for 150 families • Part of primary care team that includes a physician, nurse, and dentist • Reside in community	• Maternal deaths cut by 31% • Child deaths cut by 31%
Ethiopia	• 35,000 trained workers • Deliver family planning solutions • Provide education and care to women • Vaccinate children	• Maternal deaths cut by 50% • Child deaths cut by 26%
Malawi	• 10,000 trained workers deployed to rural regions • Educate about common childhood illness • Provide oral vaccines • Treat diarrhea, malaria, pneumonia, and other common diseases • Support mothers before, during, and after delivery	• Maternal deaths cut by 45% • Child deaths cut by 27%
Nepal	• 49,000 volunteer workers, each responsible for 100–150 families • Trained and supervised by government • Provide basic preventive care, treatment • Reside in local community	• Maternal deaths cut by 53% • Child deaths cut by 48%
Pakistan	• 100,000 trained workers • Provide family planning/basic health care • Closely supervised for quality	• Maternal deaths cut by 32% • Child deaths cut by 9%
Rwanda	• 45,000 community-selected health workers, each responsible for 100–150 households • Trained by Ministry of Health • Provide education, basic preventive care, and treatment • Distribute family planning solutions • Supported by public insurance program • Refer advanced cases to clinics	• Maternal deaths cut by 60% • Child deaths cut by 58%

Sources: Earth Institute (2011) *One Million Community Health Workers: Technical Task Force Report;* Geoghegan (2012) "Frontline Health Workers: The Best Way to Save Lives, Accelerate Progress on Global Health, and Help Advance U.S. Interests"; Earth Institute (2011) *One Million Community Health Workers: Technical Task Force Report*; Holmes (2010) "Rwanda: An Injection of Hope"; WHO (2012) *Trends in Maternal Mortality: 1990 to 2010*; UNICEF (2011) *Levels & Trends in Child Mortality Report 2011*; UNICEF (2012) *Levels & Trends in Child Mortality Report 2012*.

help the other women in the community. Though they may have assisted at the birth of many children, they often have little formal training—some may apprentice with other TBAs, but generally their skills are built over time through experience.[47]

Even when there are options for modern care, women like Sadiki, whose story appeared earlier in this chapter, prefer to use TBAs. As part of the community fabric, TBAs are generally known, respected, relied upon and trusted. Some TBAs may be linked to the formal health care sector, but for the most part they generally operate outside it. In some countries TBAs have been banned because of the perceived risk they pose to mothers and newborns due to their limited formal training and for performing deliveries outside of equipped facilities.[48]

However, for many women, particularly those in remote and rural regions, a TBA may be their only option for maternal and infant care and support. Recognizing that skills to perform specific tasks can be learned by providers, regardless of professional title, some programs are beginning to train TBAs to provide safe deliveries, while evaluating the effectiveness of their newly honed skills.[49]

A number of studies have shown that TBAs can provide good maternal and child outcomes, if they are:

- Trained and supervised
- Collaborate with other health workers
- Linked to the health infrastructure[50]

TBAs can be valuable resources to improving health care for women and children in low-resource settings with the appropriate support. Fortunately, advances in technology, such as mobile phones, may be able to play a role in facilitating their inclusion. Partnerships between TBAs, governments, and others in the private sector may help include and use TBAs as part of the solution, rather than the problem.

Franchised and Networked Health Enterprises

Bangladesh, with 150 million people, is the most densely populated large country in the world, and 40 percent of the population has no access to basic health care.[51] And with three-quarters of all births being performed without skilled assistance, it's not surprising that the country has high rates of maternal mortality (2.4 per 1,000 births) and infant mortality (38 per 1,000 births). These rates are made worse by the fact that 45 percent of women use no form of birth control, resulting in many pregnancies and births.[52]

Despite the fact that Bangladesh remains one of the world's poorest countries, about 65 percent of health care expenditures are out of pocket. Public sector community clinics provide basic care and family planning, as well as health assistants who visit homes. The public health system provides primary care, but it is mainly used for emergency and hospital-based care.[53]

The private sector comprises NGOs and microentrepreneurs, which include traditional healers, community health workers, retail pharmacists, and others providing a large proportion of outpatient treatment. For most, the pharmacy and drug sellers are generally the point of entry for people receiving any sort of health care at all.[54]

A Private Partnership Designed for Scale: The Smiling Sun Franchise Program

The Smiling Sun Franchise Program, a USAID-supported initiative, is the largest clinical social franchise program for health care in the world. By standardizing and supporting care for a group of 27 existing NGO health clinic networks—many already receiving USAID support—in 64 districts, and with 9,100 satellite sites and 6,000 community service providers, Smiling Sun is able to provide care to 15 percent of Bangladesh's population.

As a part of the network, each clinic has a similar look and feel—very clean and with the franchise's logo, a smiling sun, prominently displayed. Smiling Sun provides family planning and maternal and child care services, including contraceptives, prenatal care, labor and delivery, emergency obstetric care, postnatal care, early childhood vaccinations, pediatric evaluations, diarrheal disease treatment, malaria treatment, tuberculosis case management, pneumonia testing and treatment, STI treatment, and cervical cancer screening.

S Scaling

Some clinics, equipped with laboratory facilities and pharmacies, are able to provide a more robust suite of services. In a span of four years, the network has given over 5 million prenatal care consultations, and its skilled birth attendants assisted almost 24,000 deliveries each year between 2009 and 2011.[55]

The Smiling Sun brand maintains quality through a variety of quality control standards and processes. Quality monitoring and supervision visits track a variety of indicators and also include provider knowledge

M Maximizing Efficiency & Effectiveness

quizzes and process observations. All clinic staff members are responsible for ensuring and maintaining the quality of their services.[56]

Most people will walk into one of the 9,100 satellite clinics providing basic health services. These mobile outreach clinics are located primarily in rural regions and often set up in different places each day. Services at satellite clinics cost patients the equivalent of less than $0.50. If the workers in the satellite clinic find an advanced case, they refer the patient to a higher level of care within the system, the first stage of which would be one of the 276 "Vital" clinics.

These Vital clinics have the facilities to offer basic outpatient services and limited laboratory services. The "Ultra" clinics—of which there are forty-six—offer basic outpatient services, emergency obstetric care, and comprehensive laboratories. A single "Maxi" clinic has the most advanced facilities, laboratories, and care. The Vital, Ultra, and Maxi clinics are all run by a clinic manager and an administrative assistant, while the services are provided by physicians and paramedics, who are assisted by clinic aides and counselors. Smiling Sun also has 6,200 "salaried volunteers" who receive a $17 per month honorarium to educate their communities and refer people to the satellite clinics. They also sell water treatments, soap, safe delivery kits, pregnancy tests, zinc tablets, condoms, and other basic health products.[57]

Seeking Stability and Financial Sustainability

To stay operational, any business has to remain financially sustainable. To this end, Smiling Sun has several approaches to ensure there are both sufficient revenues and high demand for its services. Commodities are provided to the clinic for free by the government of Bangladesh, which also provides vouchers to stimulate demand. With the vouchers, which still provide only 1 percent of payments, prenatal visits are priced at about $0.40, basic pneumonia treatment at about $0.30, injectable and implantable contraceptives at about $0.50, and deliveries at about $12. Further, emergency obstetric care generates revenue, and Smiling Sun has a number of partnerships with businesses to increase revenue further.[58]

P Partner Coordination

The pricing structure also helps Smiling Sun keep a balance between sustaining services and providing care to those who cannot afford it. There are maximum and minimum price ranges that correspond to local market conditions, such as location and the existence of nearby competition. More than half of the payments for services are out of pocket, a third of services are free, about 15 percent is paid by third-parties (insurance), and, as noted, above 1 percent comes from government-provided vouchers. Program revenue covers 43 percent of program costs, with international donors supporting the remainder. Greater revenue is generated by clinics that are larger, provide a broader range of services, and are located in places with larger populations.[59]

Of course, Smiling Sun is not the only clinic social franchise. There is also Marie Stopes International's BlueStar network, which provides reproductive health services to women in Ethiopia,

Table 10 Select Social Franchising and Networked Programs for
Maternal and Child Health

Name	Country	Number of Patients	Number of Outlets
Smiling Sun— Chemonics	Bangladesh	25,324,740	9,144
Green Star	Pakistan	3,800,000	8,700
Quality Sun—PSI	Myanmar	2,120,000	1,498 (2,351 CHWs)
BlueStar—Social Marketing Co	Bangladesh	1,269,130	4,000
BlueStar—Marie Stopes	Vietnam	994,270	330
Tinh Chi Em	Vietnam	887,412	216
Confiance Network	Democratic Republic of Congo	718,351	133
RedPlan Salud— INPPARES	Peru	632,895	1,723
Merry Gold	India	536,680	478 (10,000 CHWs)
Health Keepers	Ghana	520,000	
Tunza—PSI	Kenya	440,617	258
Living Goods	Uganda	436,296	686
AMUA—Marie Stopes	Kenya	402,184	250
CFW Clinics— Health Store Foundation	Kenya and Rwanda	400,000	88

Source: Global Health Group (2012) Clinical Social Franchising Compendium.

Ghana, Madagascar, Malawi, and Vietnam. Similarly, Health
Store Foundation's CFW clinics provide maternal and child
health products and services through a franchise model. These
franchised networks provide access to critical health care products
and services while ensuring quality though the checks made by
the central organization. Each of the clinical social franchising

organizations listed in Table 10 fills a different niche in the health sector, has its own business model, and generate its own level of financial sustainability.

Mobile Technology

Mobile applications for pregnancy and delivery help facilitate distribution by communicating information to people and thereby increasing demand for health care. Mobile technologies are 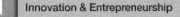 increasingly important for delivering health information to remote areas in developing countries and allow programs to easily scale and replicate across regions and cultures. Mobile phones and other telemedicine technologies can support all of the above distribution models in providing quality care, making them even more effective and efficient.

Mobile Alliance for Maternal Action (MAMA) is a public private partnership to facilitate distribution through health and nutrition text messages for expectant and new mothers. It was created in 2011 by the White House Office of Science and Technology Policy, the U.S. Department of State, the U.S. Agency for International Development (USAID), Johnson & Johnson, the United Nations Foundation, and BabyCenter, and is hosted by the mHealth Alliance. MAMA is currently being tested in Bangladesh, India, and South Africa.[60]

Expectant mothers participating in MAMA receive regular health messages on their phones regarding topics ranging from proper nutrition and safe delivery practices to breastfeeding and vaccinations. By providing health information, MAMA creates demand for health services, which in turn facilitates distribution of goods and services. The program is easy to scale and integrate into existing health care models, and can potentially have a considerable impact on maternal and infant health.[61]

Mobile technology facilitators are not strictly phone-based applications. Portable technologies now allow health workers to conduct tests in remote regions. GE's battery-powered vScan is a pocket-sized ultrasound device that takes screening and diagnostics to the poor. This device removes the travel cost that deters many people in rural areas from seeking high-level medical care that often is available only in large urban clinics.[62] Telemedicine applications are also being developed to link rural clinicians to physicians for support, guidance, and training.

Keeping Them Safe: Saving for Keeps

We now have successful systems, programs, partnerships, and organizations that have demonstrated how we can save mothers and children with basic, community-based care. Like the pharmacy on a bicycle, if patients can't go to a provider, the provider must go to them. From community health worker programs to a variety of franchise programs, we have programs that can save lives at a low cost in low-resource settings. By shifting tasks to community health workers and traditional birth attendants, and training and supporting them well, we can save millions of moms, babies, and children, even in the most remote places.

Over the past two decades, business model and technology innovations, coupled with entrepreneurial approaches from governments, NGOs, businesses, and donors, have helped increase the access, use, and quality of maternal and child health care and cut deaths of moms and babies by half. However, despite the progress, it is not yet time to celebrate. Like Sadiki's pregnancy with twins, our goal cannot be to save just one baby. Such a bittersweet outcome should only serve to strengthen our resolve to be even more innovative and more entrepreneurial to achieve all that is possible.

And that is just what Sadiki did. Following Amani's birth, she began a crusade to organize help and save others, just as she had been helped and saved. On her own initiative, she founded two women's self-help collectives where women pool their resources and start small businesses to realize their dreams.

And by the time Amani was three, Sadiki had realized a dream of her own: she opened the village's first daycare center.

Food for Thought

- What truly motivates the members of your organization? How might these motivators be incorporated into their work to foster innovative and entrepreneurial thinking and action?
- Who might be able to help you create demand for your products or services? How might you engage them in the next year?
- Which tasks might you shift to new settings to help you have greater impact? Whose buy-in might you need to help this transition go smoothly?

6

A Drop of Vinegar:
Solutions for Infectious Diseases

On the surface, David was no match for Goliath. Just a small boy in a tunic, armed only with a slingshot, yet this small boy killed a giant of a man. And so it is with infectious diseases. Minute microbes one cannot even see with the naked eye are able to kill beings much, much larger and, seemingly, more powerful than themselves—human beings like us.

Most often, however, the people they kill are poor and living in developing countries—like the Angolan soldier who contracts HIV and gives it to his wife before he dies of AIDS. Or like the baby from Zimbabwe who is bitten by a mosquito that transmits a parasite that causes a fever, then a seizure, before killing her of malaria. Or like the Indian schoolteacher who contracts HPV (human papillomavirus) on her cervix, which turns into cancer and spreads throughout her body before consuming her life. Despite the tremendous advances that have been made in the prevention and treatment of infectious diseases, people in developing countries like Angola, Zimbabwe, and India continue to fall like Goliath.

But it doesn't have to be so. We have inexpensive solutions to control infectious diseases.

A Drop of Vinegar Can Save a Life

Over half a million women each year are diagnosed with cervical cancer and more than 225,000 die of this disease. Developing countries bear the majority of the global burden.[1] Fortunately, there are new, simple, and inexpensive ways to diagnose and treat abnormal cells during the precancerous stage, killing the disease before it kills the woman. All it takes is a few drops of vinegar placed on the cervix, a cold probe, and the steady hand of a trained provider.[2] The need is huge. And the remedies are easy and cheap.

So why are women in developing countries still dying of cervical cancer?

That's exactly what Dr. Groesbeck Parham, an American gynecologic oncologist, thought when a colleague asked him to consider relocating to Africa to work. It seemed like the logical next step in his career, given his interests and passions. He had dedicated his career to providing care to some of the poorest people in the U.S.—first at Charles Drew University in south Los Angeles and later at institutions in Little Rock and Birmingham. Poverty does not end at the U.S. border, however; it widens and turns south.

So when the request came, he packed up his bags and left.

Despite the tremendous need, however, Dr. Parham found little opportunity to save women from cancer in Sub-Saharan Africa. Women arrived at his clinic too late. Even for those who arrived before their cancer had spread, the health system he found lacked sufficient pathologists, surgeons, cancer drugs, and radiation therapy to save them, and did not even have basic pain medications to relieve their suffering as their disease progressed. Most died at home, comforted only with the love of family and the certainty that their suffering would soon end.

While there were few good opportunities in Africa for cancer specialists, there were ample opportunities for AIDS experts. By 2005, money for AIDS was beginning to pour into Africa through the Global Fund to Combat HIV, Malaria and Tuberculosis (Global Fund), and the President's Emergency Program for AIDS Relief (PEPFAR). Clinical and technical professionals who were expert in

Cervical Cancer: Diagnosis and Treatment in Developing Countries

Cervical cancer is caused by a sexually transmitted virus, the human papillomavirus (HPV), which is so common that most sexually active women get it at some point in their lives.[3] Women with weakened immune systems, such as those who have HIV, have a harder time getting rid of HPV. In fact, women with HIV are four to five times more likely to contract cervical cancer. Unfortunately, most women in developing countries generally do not have access to Pap smears, the laboratory test that has helped significantly diminish cervical cancer deaths in developed countries.[4]

HPV can lead to abnormal cells on the cervix, which, if untreated, can become cancerous and lead to a slow, painful death. Fortunately, visual inspection with acetic acid (VIA) can diagnose cancerous and precancerous growths, and it is elegantly simple to do. During a pelvic exam, a trained nurse, or another nonphysician health care provider, washes the cervix with a small amount of household vinegar (acetic acid). Changes associated with precancerous and some cancer growths will appear as white lesions, and the vast majority can be treated on the spot with a cold match probe.[5]

HIV clinical care, prevention, program development, research design, monitoring, and evaluation—anything AIDS related—were being actively recruited. That prompted Dr. Parham's colleague Dr. Jeffrey Stringer, an HIV specialist from the University of Alabama, to move to Zambia and help start the Centre for Infectious Disease Research, Zambia (CIDRZ).

Dr. Parham and his colleagues eventually received a small grant to study the rate of HPV infection among Zambian women with AIDS.[6] Until that point, most studies had identified rates of precancerous cervical lesion at between 20 and 25 percent of the sample. However, among HIV-positive Zambian women, Dr. Parham found that almost all (94 percent) had precancerous lesions.[7] This shocking finding drew international attention and prompted the Centers for Disease Control to fund a pilot cervical cancer prevention and treatment program in Zambia for women with HIV. This program was the world's first cervical cancer prevention program linked to HIV care and treatment and has become a model program, training providers throughout Africa.[8]

The first task at hand for Dr. Parham was to figure out how he and Dr. Mwanahamhuntu, the clinic's only other doctor, could see all the patients who needed their care. The only feasible way was to train nurses to do it and to supervise them well. This had been done with HIV treatment, and it had worked.[9] Initially, quality control was easy since the screening clinics were nearby. However, as they began to place more nurses in clinics around the country, they had to come up with a better way.

The answer came in a conversation with a colleague from PATH, a large Seattle-based NGO. PATH does health care innovation in seventy countries, and it was trying to solve a similar problem in China. The solution was for nurses to take a digital photograph of the cervix after the vinegar was placed on it. 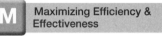 Dr. Parham later connected the camera to a computer that allowed the photograph to be immediately magnified to twenty times its actual size, allowing both the nurse and the patient to clearly see any lesion prior to treatment.[10]

For quality control, all cervical photographs and treatment decisions were electronically sent to the central hospital, where doctors could review them at a later time. However, if a nurse needed an immediate consultation, she simply sent the doctor a text message. He could then download the photo on his smartphone and text a response. And all of this could happen while the patient was still in the examination room. This new procedure dramatically increased the ability of doctors to provide clinical supervision and oversight of patient care to nurses at multiple clinics.

The photographs were also useful for training purposes. The doctors and nurses reviewed all photographs on a weekly basis as a group, and over time their agreement about the diagnosis increased from 75 percent to nearly 100 percent. The nurses were now as accurate in their assessments as the seasoned doctors.[11]

While Dr. Parham has been one of the champions for calling attention to cervical cancer and working to combat it in Zambia, he certainly wasn't working alone. He was joined and supported by a number of colleagues and friends throughout the country in clinical, government, busi- 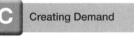 ness, and community settings. He had a strong Zambian team,[12] and when a fellow gynecologist, Dr. Christine Keseba, became the First Lady of Zambia in 2011, she used her position to encourage women to get screened and for public and private partners to increase access to affordable cervical cancer screening. In addition, demand in the community was boosted by the team's cancer and women's health advocates, who led community awareness campaigns and provided community-based support to patients.

Rather than build a stand-alone program in partnership with the Ministry of Health, the program was integrated into the HIV programs. This enabled the program to quickly increase access to care for women who were at highest risk. It also reduced infrastructure costs. All local staff were Ministry of Health per- 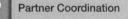 sonnel, helping ensure sustainability and government commitment to the program. Patients who needed additional services were referred within the public health system, further integrating the care system.

Across the globe, Dr. Parham received ideas, support, and money from colleagues throughout Africa, Asia, Europe, and North and South America. The clinical leaders he trained throughout Africa became the technical expert advisors to help develop Pink

Ribbon Red Ribbon, a public-private partnership to combat cervical and breast cancer. The partners committed $85 million to the effort. Engagement by the business community in health efforts such as these is not only the right thing to do, it makes good business sense.

Pink Ribbon Red Ribbon: A Public-Private Partnership to Combat Cervical and Breast Cancer

Pink Ribbon Red Ribbon is an innovative partnership to leverage public and private investments in global health to combat cervical and breast cancer—two of the leading causes of cancer death in women—in developing nations in Sub-Saharan Africa and Latin America. Led by the George W. Bush Institute, the U.S. President's Emergency Plan for AIDS Relief (PEPFAR), Susan G. Komen for the Cure, and the Joint United Nations Programme on HIV/AIDS (UNAIDS), Pink Ribbon Red Ribbon expands the availability of vital cervical cancer screening and treatment—especially for high-risk HIV-positive women—and also promotes breast cancer education. Pink Ribbon Red Ribbon partners also work to de-stigmatize cancers and thereby lessen the shame that women with cancer experience; shame that prevents them from getting care early.

The partnership leverages the platform and resources of PEPFAR, established under President Bush and a cornerstone of President Obama's Global Health Initiative (GHII). The partners include Merck and GSK, the pharmaceutical firms that manufacture the commercially available vaccines that can prevent HPV infection in most cases; Becton Dickinson, a multinational supplier of medical equipment, supplies, and technologies; Caris Life Sciences, a pathology diagnostic firm; QIAGEN, the firm that manufactures careHPV, an HPV diagnostic test; the Bristol Myers Squibb Foundation; and IBM. The Pink Ribbon Red Ribbon partners and others provide technical guidance, advocacy, and donated or discounted products and services to help countries combat cervical and breast cancer.[13]

New Solutions for Cervical Cancer

The doctors in Zambia were not the only or the first ones to work on this problem.[14] Nor has their innovative approach been the only method tried and tested. With financial support from the Gates Foundation, PATH created a partnership with Digene
(now QIAGEN, a corporation
that develops and markets diagnostic tests), to develop a new low-cost test to detect HPV DNA. Their product, careHPV, allows for screening of women en masse—a whole village or community at a time.

With visual inspection with acetic acid (VIA), providers must test each woman one by one. It's a good option when testing populations who are known to be at high risk for HPV, such as women with HIV. However, all sexually active women are at risk for developing cervical cancer, and the vast majority will not have HIV. In certain contexts it may be more efficient to screen large groups of women for HPV and then do VIA on just the women who are found to be positive for HPV. This method shifts the procedure from the provider to the patient.

With careHPV, cells from the vagina are collected with a soft brush-like applicator, placed in a container, and taken to a laboratory. The procedure can be done by a provider in a clinic as well as by a patient in the privacy of her home. Only if the sample is positive will she be required to have the VIA procedure. Once approved for self-collection of the sample by the patient, this product may be able to reduce the workload of providers significantly.[15]

In addition, the potential to dramatically reduce cervical cancer deaths in developing countries in the future received a major boost when the GAVI Alliance, the public–private partnership discussed in chapter 4 that helps countries stimulate demand for vaccines, agreed to work with developing countries to prepare for the introduction and scale-up of the vaccine against HPV. GAVI estimates that through its support, more than 30 million girls will be immunized against HPV by 2020.[16]

Since the Zambian Ministry of Health's cervical cancer program was launched in 2006, almost 100,000 women have been screened for cervical cancer, and it is beginning an HPV vaccination campaign with support from Merck. In addition, over 200 health care professionals from ten African countries have been trained in cervical cancer screening and treatment in Zambia. The cervical cancer prevention program has thus far been replicated in eight of them.[17]

Aids for Controlling AIDS

The progress that is being made in fighting cervical cancer builds off the progress that has been made in HIV/AIDS care and leverages its vast infrastructure. In less than a decade, the number of new HIV infections each year decreased nearly 15 percent, while the number of people on antiretrovirals skyrocketed more than twenty-three-fold.[18]

But without continued commitment, the gains made may be short-lived. HIV/AIDS has been devastating communities around the world for several decades, taking the lives of nearly 1.5 million people each year—more than 25 million people in the past thirty years.[19] Sub-Saharan Africa is the hardest-hit region, accounting for over two-thirds of the 34 million people affected by AIDS, though it has only 15 percent of the world's population.[20]

Despite the magnitude of the problem, and despite the hurdles and setbacks, we have made significant strides in combating HIV/AIDS across the globe. Over 8 million people now receive antiretroviral treatment (ARVs), dramatically extending lives.[21] In addition, ARV treatments that cost $10,000 per year when they first appeared and were horribly complicated to use are now incredibly simple combination ARVs, and most basic regimens cost less than 4% their original price in developing countries. This achievement was due to the efforts of many public and private partners to push down drug prices, including pharmaceutical entrepreneurs in Brazil and China, the Clinton Health Access Initiative, and UNITAID.[22] In addition, the simplified combination ARVs made it easier for patients to stay adherent, which improves outcomes.[23] This simplification has also made it possible to shift the administration of ARVs to nurses in rural communities.

With the creation of antiretroviral drugs, solutions to combat HIV exist, but not everyone is getting treated. Seven million people in low- and middle-income countries still do not receive any sort of treatment for HIV, including 44 percent of those in Sub-Saharan Africa, 56 percent of people in Asia, 77 percent of people in Eastern Europe and Central Asia, and 87 percent of people in the Middle East.[24]

To increase the reach of programs, HIV care can be integrated into primary medical care, which creates synergies, reduces redundancies, and helps ensure sustainability. In Zambia, for example, integrated care has re- sulted in an increase in the new cases of HIV identified. If you are at a clinic for some other health problem, you may be willing to be tested for HIV while you're there. This may increase the chance that more patients can be tested, since the stigma associated with coming in to be tested specifically for HIV is reduced. When HIV testing was done in the general medical sector in Zambia, 53 to 58 percent of those who came in for other health issues accepted HIV testing; 13 to 24 percent of those tested were found to be HIV positive.[25]

Integrating HIV into general medical services in Mozambique resulted in improved HIV testing, increased efficiency in getting people on ARVs, better patient compliance, and more geographic access to HIV services.[26] The benefits are significant, which suggests that integration of HIV into general medical services may provide an effective path to success. However, general primary care services are often short-staffed and underfunded.[27] Task-shifting, so that basic checkups and medication refills are more efficiently performed, and using checklists, which improves compliance, efficiency, and quality of care, could solve these problems. Task shifting to the general medical system could take place without imposing great costs on the system, improving both the general health care system and HIV care, provided that safeguards are in place.

While there have been significant advances in HIV prevention and treatment, there remain significant challenges that can be addressed with our *IMPACTS* approach. Task shifting of antiretroviral treatments from doctors to nurses has been successful. In order to scale up access to care, treatment must now be shifted from HIV specialty sectors to the general medical sector.[28]

Champions have been critical in helping to create demand for controlling HIV throughout the world. When Americans think of who or what has helped call attention to HIV, depending on their age, they may think of Magic Johnson, Ryan White, the AIDS Coalition to Unleash Power (ACT UP!), or a teacher, a parent, a minister, a friend, a movie, or 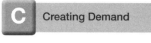 a TV show. Likewise, when Africans think of HIV leaders, they may mention President George W. Bush, who initiated PEPFAR, or Nkosi Johnson, a South African boy born with AIDS, who was keynote speaker at the International AIDS Conference in Durban, South Africa, in 2000. He ended his speech with the statement: "Care for us and accept us—we are all human beings. We are normal. We have hands. We have feet. We can walk, we can talk, we have needs just like everyone else—don't be afraid of us—we are all the same!"[29] Nkosi helped put a face on AIDS in Africa and stimulated more calls for action and treatment among Africans before he died at the age of twelve.

Some attribute the progress that has been made in the control of infectious diseases to the fact that there have been champions, and the lack of similar progress in other areas such as noncommunicable disease to the lack of champions. Champions have been needed at all levels to create demand, stimulate supply, encourage innovation, build new markets, increase access, improve quality, and lower costs. To reduce deaths and dramatically increase access to care for the poor, new leaders will be needed to call attention to the problem and to show the way.

Mobile Technology

The use of mobile technology to greatly improve access and quality control has been key in controlling infectious disease amid a variety of conditions. It has been used to improve HIV prevention efforts; disease diagnoses, care, and treatment; maternal labor and delivery; vaccination rates; and child health outcomes in low-resource settings.[30] In developing countries, mobile technology has been a critical component of task shifting, reducing medication stockouts, and confirming the provenance of medications.[31]

One of the most difficult problems with malaria control is ensuring that medications are available where and when they are needed—often a major problem in hard-to-reach rural areas that may run out of supplies before the next shipment arrives. Very sick patients can't get well if they can't get their medications, and donors lose confidence. To solve these problems in Tanzania, SMS for Life, a public-private partnership among Novartis, IBM, Vodafone, the Roll Back Malaria Partnership, and the Ministry of Health and Social Welfare of Tanzania, was developed.[32] Clinics are sent weekly staff reminders to check for supplies of malaria medications. Clinic staff responds with the requested information, and they are rewarded for doing so with free airtime on their cell phones.

The centrally stored information then allows the central manager to modify future delivery of supplies to the clinic or to send additional supplies before the next planned delivery. The program has reduced stockouts for all malaria medications in 129 health facilities from 78 percent to 26 percent per month over twenty-one weeks.[33] The project was so successful that it is now being used by more than 5,000 clinics in Tanzania, and it has been expanded to additional countries and to include the monitoring of many critically important health supplies.[34] An effort in Uganda enhanced this system by crowd-sourcing stockouts. It allows patients to anonymously text in if they experienced a stockout when they sought care. This type of crowd sourcing not only engages and gives communities voice, but creates a way of alerting health officials when essential medicines are missing.[35]

Another important application of mobile phone technology is ensuring the quality of medications. Counterfeit medication is a big problem in many developing nations. Each year 700,000 people die because they are given medications that look real but are substandard. It is estimated that counterfeit medications account for 35 percent to 75 percent of medications for some conditions consumed in lower-income countries.[36] At best, a patient remains ill. At worst, the patient spreads an infectious disease to many others before dying. To combat this problem, a consortium of African telecom operators, pharmaceutical associations, technology companies, and philanthropies created the mPedigree Network.

With mPedigree, a verification sticker is placed on the back of legitimate medications. Prior to purchasing the medication, the patient scratches off the sticker and sends a text message to a secure server to verify that the medication is legitimate. Once the medication has been verified, the patient then purchases it. Other companies that also have text-message verification systems include PharmaSecure, Kezzler, and Sproxil. This initiative has been rolled out in many developing countries.

Rapid Diagnostics for Infectious Diseases

The VIA procedure takes a nurse only five minutes to determine whether a woman may have precancerous cervical lesions and enables her to be treated on the spot. Similarly, rapid diagnostic tests (RDTs) have greatly increased the ability to shift the tasks of diagnosing and treating many conditions and diseases from high-skilled personnel to lower-skilled ones and from clinical settings to nonclinical ones. Like home pregnancy tests, the ready availability of these tests greatly facilitates the ability to diagnose disease in local communities where people live.

There are now rapid diagnostic tests for over thirty conditions, including malaria, HIV, syphilis, tuberculosis, and hepatitis B.[37] The rapid diagnostic tests for infectious diseases are generally very easy to use, require little training, and can facilitate on-the-spot treatment. Some do require subtle interpretations; however, a group at UCLA has developed a smartphone application to help take out the guesswork for some tests.[38]

RTDs are generally more expensive than traditional tests, and their costs are often prohibitive in very low-resource settings (see Table 11). However, with the growing demand for rapid diagnostic tests due to task shifting from clinics to community settings, it is likely more manufacturers will enter the market, increasing competition and introducing economies of scale that may reduce prices and improve access.

Table 11 Advantages and Disadvantages of Rapid Diagnostic Tests

Advantages	Disadvantages
• Easy to use • Little training is generally required • Immediate or same-day results are available, often allowing people to be treated on the spot • Shelf life of one–two years • Some may not need to be refrigerated	• Cost is generally higher than traditional tests • Good distribution systems are needed so they don't expire before use • Subjective interpretation of results is required • Some are not as sensitive as traditional tests • Good quality-control systems are necessary

Source: RDTinfo, "Tests for Specific Diseases."

Goliath Gets Up

We have inexpensive solutions to control infectious diseases. People in developing countries do not have to fall like Goliath. Whether it's a drop of vinegar or integrating specialized services into the general health care system, solutions do exist and can be brought to those who most need access to high-quality care at low cost. As with any disease, the first choice should be to take preventive measures, such as encouraging use of condoms to reduce the spread of HIV and other sexually transmitted diseases. The number of rapid diagnostics is increasing, and mobile technologies are being used to enable task shifting while maintaining quality of care. All of this is making it increasingly possible to task-shift, scale up, and spread out health care to improve access, quality, and use, all while reducing costs. The *IMPACTS* approach will help us bridge the final mile in health care to finally defeat the scourge of infectious diseases ravaging the developing world.

Food for Thought

- What three organizations might help you achieve greater impact or scale (including government, NGOs, businesses, donors, and others)? How might you also help them? How might you engage them in this work over the next year?
- What might you do to ensure that the quality of shifted tasks remains high (for example, training, supervision, mobile phone applications, checklists, or incentives)? How will you know if you've succeeded?

7

The Elephants in the Room: Noncommunicable Diseases

Noncommunicable diseases (NCDs), including cardiovascular diseases (stroke and heart attack), mental illness, cancer (but not cervical cancer), chronic lung diseases, and diabetes, represent nearly two-thirds of all deaths worldwide. Eighty percent of NCD cases occur in low and middle-income countries.[1] They will result in a potential loss of $47 trillion worldwide over the twenty years from 2010 to 2030—the equivalent of 75 percent of the global GDP in 2010—if nothing is done to stop them. Cardiovascular diseases and mental illnesses alone will account for 70 percent of that loss.[2] Regardless of how we measure it, in terms of lives or money lost, NCDs are costly. Yet for the most part, they are ignored, especially in developing countries.

They are the elephants in the room.

The tremendously negative impact of noncommunicable diseases on global health prompted the United Nations in 2011 to convene a high-level meeting of world leaders to develop a consensus to combat them. The only other health problem that has warranted such action by the United Nations was AIDS.

Noncommunicable diseases are problems in all countries, regardless of income. However, for a variety of reasons, as we shall see, some of the most effective and efficient ways of addressing these problems may come from low- and middle-income countries.

Serious as a Heart Attack

The most common cause of death in the world is cardiovascular disease. Each year, stroke kills 5.87 million people, and heart attacks kill an additional 7 million. Those who don't die immediately are often left severely disabled.[3] All of these are not just preventable deaths—they are easily preventable deaths. By decreasing tobacco use and salt intake and by increasing exercise and improving diets, most of these deaths can be avoided. A small dose of daily aspirin and generic antihypertensive might prevent or reduce risk for the remainder.[4]

Most cardiovascular disease risk factors are related to lifestyle, highly dependent upon behavior, and affected by social networks. A person's risk for becoming obese may increase by nearly 60 percent if friends gain weight; a similar correlation is found on the impact of social networks on smoking behavior.[5]

This is an area that providers who are part of the local community, know the local culture, work with families in their homes, and are respected and trusted may be particularly helpful and skilled. Task shifting to community providers and settings, which has been shown to be cost effective in improving health outcomes for mothers and children, can be leveraged to improve health outcomes for entire families.[6]

Community health workers can play integral roles in modifying behaviors within communities. These behavioral interventions can include not only habits like hand washing, breastfeeding, and using bed nets. They can also be trained to take blood pressure, monitor weight, encourage exercise and appropriate diet, and discourage smoking. Health workers actively involved in the community can also serve as positive role models and help change strongly held health beliefs that often prevent community members from using lifesaving health care solutions.[7]

Changing behaviors requires community and social support, modification of the environment and, at times, regulatory nudges. However, when prevention does not work and one needs advanced care, that too can be done efficiently in low-resource settings.

Using a Head to Save a Heart:
The Case of Narayana Hrudayalaya

Dr. Devi Shetty believes that *where* you live should not determine *whether* you live. However, far too often that is exactly the case, as he witnessed in his native India and in Great Britain, where he trained to be a cardiac surgeon. In England people would be treated with medication when they experienced angina chest pain caused by inadequate oxygen supply to the heart. And when the medication did not work or the disease was already too advanced, he could perform a coronary artery bypass procedure or an angioplasty to increase blood flow to the heart. This would help them avoid a heart attack and live healthy lives. In India, however, such chest pain would often be a sure harbinger of death if medication treatment didn't work because most patients were unable to afford the expensive surgical options.

Dr. Shetty recognized, however, that there were tremendous inefficiencies in cardiac surgery—not just in India, but throughout the world. If he could reduce this inefficiency, he could treat many more people in the same amount of time. The cost of services would fall, access 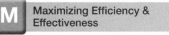 would increase, and many more lives could be saved. But could he make increasing access to care for the poor financially sustainable? He could and he did. By focusing on the process of care, Dr. Shetty did what he intended: he innovatively created a new way to deliver high-quality, high-precision health care to the poor while generating a profit.[8]

Narayana Hrudayalaya (NH), the hospital network Dr. Shetty founded in Bangalore, India, in 2001, has become one of the world's largest cardiovascular groups. Its largest cardiac facility has 1,000 beds and performs over thirty major heart surgeries per day. In total, the network of hospitals has performed more than 50,000 since its founding.[9] Dr. Shetty reduces costs by maximizing efficiency and treating high numbers of patients. Each NH surgeon generally performs only specific types of surgical procedures. Patient-related or back-office work is task-shifted whenever possible to nurses, clerks, or technicians.[10]

NH is a for-profit hospital network. Those who have insurance or cash, pay. Those who do not, don't. NH is able do this by offering different levels of accommodation and attention outside the operating room—rather like passengers on an airplane, one 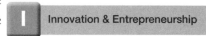 flying first class and another in coach. Both passengers leave and arrive at their destination at the same time. They just have different levels of comforts—seat size, food options, boarding order, and in-flight entertainment. But those who can't afford first-class amenities still get to their destinations safely.

NH uses tiered services and amenities (time, rooms, surgeon, and so forth) to create different price tiers. Those who want better amenities, such as air-conditioned, private rooms, pay a premium. And just like an airline, the highest level of service generates much more profit per person served than do lower levels of service.

By maintaining a careful balance of service type, NH can service the poor and not only be financially sustainable but highly profitable. NH is known for such high quality that the hospital attracts medical tourists—people from wealthier countries who come to NH in India because such care is either not available or affordable. For NH provides not only high-quality care, but provides it at a fraction of the cost of its competitors, even in India. The average cost of heart surgery at NH is about 30 percent of the price charged elsewhere in India and only 5 to 10 percent of that charged in the United States.[11]

The hospital has goals of how many poor people it should serve. And since it can only provide care to the poor based upon the profit it makes from others, it carefully monitors its patient flow, revenue, expenses, and return on investment. In fact, 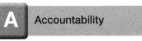 each day, surgeons receive statements that show their billable procedures from the previous day, as well as their costs to the system. The doctors can then make decisions on how best to plan their patient flows to meet targets.[12]

NH not only shifts tasks from doctors to nurses and technicians, but also shifts tasks from its cardiac specialty hospital to general hospitals and providers via telemedicine. NH has seventeen coronary units located in remote hospitals, where emer- 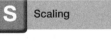 gency cases are treated. In addition, it supports over 100 facilities in India and over 50 facilities in Africa—for free. Doctors in other developing countries can receive consultations on cases from NH doctors via telemedicine. In the past ten years, NH has treated over 50,000 patients through its telemedicine services. The technology has also been used to provide remote education and training sessions. Such relationships may facilitate referrals to NH from these countries for patients who can afford it.[13]

Partnerships have also allowed NH to scale beyond cardiac care to other diseases, including cancer, diabetes, dentistry, and ophthalmology. Its processes in these other specialty hospitals follow the same approach to efficiency used by the cardiac 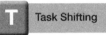 hospitals, and they also share common infrastructure.[14] This allows each hospital to realize the benefits of specialization and economies of scale simultaneously. The hospital's multidisciplinary network also allows patients with various conditions to remain within a single system they trust— after all, the woman you treat successfully for hypertension today may have precancerous cervical lesions tomorrow. If so, she'll know where to go to get the care that she needs at prices she can afford.

NH has also created an insurance scheme that provides health coverage for only pennies a month by partnering with the government. The program engages businesses, cooperatives, and other organizations to enroll their entire staff or membership for a low premium. Since the likelihood of needing intensive surgery was less than a tenth of a percent, the scheme was able to fund itself by enrolling large groups. Realizing that the program would increase demand for services, hospitals agreed to the lower negotiated rates that were a part of the scheme. The insurance program has allowed the poor access to quality services at a very affordable price, all while paying for itself.[15]

Recently, NH has partnered with Ascension Health, a faith-based nonprofit health organization in the U.S., to scale its high-quality service in the Cayman Islands—a quick 50-minute flight from Miami. The goal of the partnership is to become a medical tourism hotspot by replicating the high-quality, low-cost care NH has provided in India. The $2 billion project will include a multi-specialty hospital with 2,000 beds.[16]

NH creates local demand by doing community outreach and helping people learn if they are at risk. NH conducts outreach camps to reach remote communities and screen patients for cardiac diagnosis and care. Cardiologists and technicians use mobile vans equipped with ECG machines, defibrillators, and other equipment to conduct these outreach camps. Screenings are conducted at no cost to the patients and are funded by charitable organizations. Any patient needing advanced care is referred to NH hospitals.[17]

By conducting this outreach, NH improves access to quality care in remote communities that otherwise would not receive it. As discussed earlier, NH generated international demand on the basis of its reputation as a low-cost, high-quality provider, through telemedicine connections and its many international partners.

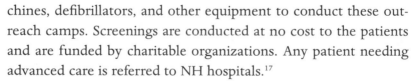
C   Creating Demand

Seeing Possibilities: Eye Surgery for the Poor— The Aravind Eye Center

NH has been a very successful private, for-profit company that provides advanced and specialized health care for the poor, and its model can be replicated for other highly common diseases in densely populated areas. Its ability to bring efficient, high-quality, low-cost advanced care to the poor builds on a model shown to be effective by an NGO, the Aravind Eye Center. Like Dr. Shetty of NH, Dr. G. Venkataswamy, or "Dr. V," as he was known, also wanted to improve care to the poor in a financially sustainable way. He knew that the government alone couldn't do so by itself, so he founded the Aravind Eye Care System, an NGO to address the huge problem of vision impairment in India.

Aravind Eye Hospitals is the largest eye care provider in the world, with 2.8 million outpatient visits; it performs over 340,000 surgeries annually. Aravind provides services to the rich and poor alike: some 60 percent of these surgeries are services to the poor at reduced prices or for free.[18] It greatly improves access to high-quality eye care for the populations it serves in a way that is acceptable, affordable, and financially sustainable. How can this be done?

Aravind relies on an assembly-line production system to perform cataract surgery. For example, when a surgeon finishes with one patient, the next one is already anesthetized, waiting only for the surgeon to put on new sterile garb and begin. Likewise, all movements in surgery are essentially choreographed. Virtually every movement and need is anticipated by the surgical assistants in order to maximize efficiency and effectiveness.

This assembly-line approach not only enables the system to provide care for many more patients, it also develops highly skilled surgical staff. As a result, complications are rare, and when they occur they are quickly remedied.[19] Through mass marketing and eye screening camps, Aravind helps generate demand for its services. Quality is carefully developed and monitored, but specialization reinforces this goal, with the surgeons performing more than ten times as many surgeries as other doctors, leading to more experience and higher quality—all facilitated by a system designed for efficiency.

Operational costs are kept low by use of lean operations and other system efficiencies. Aravind even manufactures its own intraocular lenses to control both costs and quality. In addition to keeping costs down, patients who can afford to pay for care receive additional perks to in-

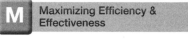 **M** Maximizing Efficiency & Effectiveness

crease their comfort. People who can afford to pay often have many other options for eye care, but choose Aravind due to the reputation for high quality. The higher fees paid by those who can afford them helps Aravind to provide low-cost or free services to the poor and remain financially sustainable.

If you are reading this book and are from a developed country like the United States, you are probably doing so with the help of corrective lenses. In fact, two out of three people in the U.S. use corrective lenses.[20] Without them, activities that are basic to our lives, like driving or working, would be nearly impossible. And vision is the primary way we engage with the world and identify others. Without it we would be socially handicapped. Even if we knew with whom we were speaking, we might be unable to read subtle facial cues and react in socially appropriate ways.

Vision impairment and blindness are enormous problems around the world. There are nearly 300 million people in the world who are visually impaired, a population nearly the size of the U.S.[21] Moreover, 90 percent of them live in developing countries. The visually impaired and those who have to care for them have higher levels of unemployment, increased welfare costs, and fewer educational opportunities. By solving problems of visual impairment, we will see increased independence, self-esteem, and participation in social networks, less poverty and hunger, and decreased gender inequality.[22]

Aravind is combating vision impairment in India by providing highly efficient, high-quality care for the poor through efficiencies and a financially diverse patient pool similar to NH's. Further, Aravind manufactures its own lenses to reduce costs for its prescription eyeglasses and cataract surgeries. Community outreach screening camps improve access, with the mobile clinics screening patients in local communities and referring advanced cases to Aravind's main facility when needed.

Eyeglasses for the Poor: VisionSpring

Though the majority of people who suffer from visual impairment are over fifty, 19 million children under fifteen suffer from visual impairment, and over 60 percent of these can be easily diagnosed and their eyesight corrected with glasses. In fact, glasses could help 43 percent of visually impaired people.[23] VisionSpring, an NGO operating in India, Bangladesh, El Salvador, and South Africa, uses a microfranchise model to bring vision screening and glasses to those who need them. VisionSpring has sold over 1 million pairs of eyeglasses since 2001 by training local individuals to create their own businesses in screening patients and supplying them with eyeglasses to sell.[24]

VisionSpring entrepreneurs get a "Business in a Bag" with the supplies needed to get started and a brief training on eye care. The entrepreneurs then provide community education, screen- 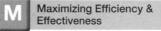 ings, and opportunities for people to buy ready-made glasses for less than $4. If someone proves to have a more complex vision impairment, he or she is referred to a more skilled provider.[25]

VisionSpring trains its entrepreneurs to test customers' eyesight by using a very simple method. The entrepreneur asks the potential customer to hold one end of a string. With the other end in hand to measure distance, the salesperson walks 10 feet away and holds up a small sign. The customer is then asked to read the symbols of varying sizes on the sign. Based on the responses, the entrepreneur determines which of her premanufactured glasses are most suitable for her customer's eyes and offers a pair for less

than $4. And while the glasses are indeed limited in the kinds of
lenses available, VisionSpring is sensitive to the fact that even if
they need to see, people still want to look good. If they are going
to sell glasses, they are going to have to be low cost, fashionable,
and effective—and they are.

VisionSpring anticipates selling a million eyeglasses in 2012, as
many glasses as the organization sold in the previous ten years.
It has also increased its reach
by developing a fee-for-service
franchise model to disseminate
sales kits to existing for-profit and nonprofit organizations. Vision-
Spring discovered that a bottleneck in its ability to scale was its
focus on serving the vision technician/entrepreneurs it trained to
distribute its products.

To increase its ability to scale in developing countries, it began shifting the distribution of its products to entrepreneurs and
NGOs that have their own distribution networks. For example,
there are many local entrepreneurs already established in rural
communities. They know the people, the culture, and the businesses. These distribution entrepreneurs can then partner with
local established businesses to test vision and sell glasses to the
businesses' employees. In some cases, the cost of the glasses may
be fully or partially subsidized by the employer, since a worker
who can see better can be more productive. Such coordinated
partnerships can create wins for everyone—for the employer, for
the entrepreneur, and for the patients.

Through partnerships with organizations such as BRAC,
VisionSpring can sell glasses to millions of people. BRAC also
has health volunteers who do
outreach in communities and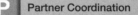
who can sell these glasses as
part of that work. This creates a win–win for both: VisionSpring
distributes its products and BRAC adds a new service. And since
BRAC has a larger portfolio, it is more likely to reach many more
people.[26]

Of course, BRAC is hardly the only way VisionSpring can get its product out. As we saw in chapter 6, Smiling Sun in Bangladesh sees 25 million patients per year and has over 9,000 outlets.[27] Though it is overseen by a nonprofit, the vendors are for-profit entrepreneurs, as are the CFW Clinics in Rwanda and Kenya. The franchisor manages procurement for the franchisees as well as logistics. Through partnerships with these types of organizations, VisionSpring can benefit from filling large-scale purchases, while partnering organizations receive low-cost eyeglasses, enabling both to be more sustainable.

Community health workers around the world can be a part of addressing vision impairment. Nepal has nearly 50,000 volunteer community workers and Rwanda, 45,000. These workers have incentives to see patients and ensure that they receive good care. Procurement is handled by their governments, which also control the entire public health care delivery systems—clinics, hospital, mobile units—all vehicles through which very inexpensive eyewear could be sold and distributed, again creating a win–win for everyone.[28]

High-Access and High-Quality Health Care for the Poor: Can We Have Both?

VisionSpring and Aravind are good examples of our ability to provide high-access and high-quality care in low-cost and appropriate ways. Though custom-made eyeglasses provide more precise vision correction than ready-to-wear lenses, for the vast majority of people who are otherwise unable to see clearly, these low-cost ready-to-wear glasses are an excellent option. They enable people who need corrective lenses but who are very poor to improve their vision in order to get an education, work, and be productive members of their communities.

However, VisionSpring cannot be the only option for the poor with impaired vision. A subset of people with impaired vision will have treatable medical conditions, such as glaucoma or cataracts, that are causing their vision impairment. Such conditions require the attention of providers with far greater clinical skills than a smart microentrepreneur skilled at selling ready-made glasses to manual laborers on their way to work, village women in the marketplace, and children in the schoolyard. These higher-skilled providers must also be available. And as we've seen through the example of Aravind, high-quality specialty eye care for those who need it can still be provided at low cost when done efficiently.

In many settings and for many diseases, we do not have to choose whether to provide high access or high quality. By consistently being innovative and entrepreneurial, we can provide them both—at low cost and in appropriate ways.

Care for the Least of These: Community-Based Care for Depression

Depression can creep up on you slowly or seem to attack you all of a sudden. It can make you feel tired and restless, yet keep you from sleeping. It can eat your appetite, consume you in shame, and cloud your thinking. Regardless of whether you're thinking of the past, the present, or the future, you may feel only sadness and despair and wonder if life is worth living. This is how depression is experienced by many of the 350 million people that it affects worldwide each year.[29]

Depression is a leading cause of number of years of life lost due to disability in the world.[30] This is true for both men and women, but for women, it's twice as common. Its subtle symptoms—irritability, loss of appetite, depressed mood, difficulty concentrating, loss of energy, insomnia, feeling slowed, feeling guilty—seem all too common, something that everyone gets every once in a while. It's just that for the depressed, the feelings linger.

Like high blood pressure, diabetes, or cancer, depression is a biological disorder. Depression affects the brain and can be triggered by a host of genetic, biological, environmental, and psychological factors. Yet its impact is far-reaching, particularly for people in developing countries, who generally have no access to formal mental health care. Though people may outwardly appear normal, their work and family life are significantly impaired. Depression makes it difficult to survive, particularly in places where survival is already difficult.[31]

And many don't. It is estimated that nearly 900,000 otherwise healthy people commit suicide each year.[32] Fortunately depression is easily preventable with the systems we already have in place in developing countries and can be scaled.

Multiple studies conducted in developing countries throughout the world have shown that depression can be effectively treated by trained lay practitioners, counselors, and health workers within the community setting.[33] In Pakistan such care was ef- fectively provided by the same community health workers who provide community-based care to women and their families (see chapter 5).[34] Therapy groups may be particularly effective in some settings as it may not only help to greatly increase access where there are a limited number of providers, but may also be viewed as an extension of traditional social structures and networks.[35]

Providers are generally trained over the course of a couple of months and do not even need a background in health. Like all community health workers, lay mental health providers require regular supervision by more experienced mental health providers to maintain quality control. Supervision can be provided in person and, when that is not feasible, by phone.

Like other health workers, lay mental health counselors should be linked to more experienced providers and systems to which they can refer more severely depressed patients for more intensive treatment, such as medication or hospitalization when it is indicated and available. In addition, there are also a wide variety of effective, inexpensive, and easy-to-use medications available in developing countries that can treat depression either alone or in combination with a variety of talk therapies. Many of these medications can be prescribed by trained nurses or, in some settings, by trained pharmacists.

The Rwandan Defense Force:
Warriors for Health

Soldiers may be at particularly high risk for mental health problems, given their prolonged exposure to dangerous and violent situations. However, they may be reluctant to seek travel permission to get care due to military cultural and male social norms that may view a mental health problem as a sign of weakness and unreliability, unfitting for a soldier or man. To cope with this stress, many soldiers turn to alcohol, unprotected sex, violence, or other maladaptive behaviors that only compound their problems.[36]

To reduce barriers to mental health care and to scale up services, the Rwandan Defense Force has begun task-shifting mental health care from social workers to peer-counselors who live in the same settings and are selected by the very soldiers who seek their care. With support from Charles Drew University, PEPFAR, and the Rwandan government, peer-counselors receive three weeks of intensive training that includes mental health counseling, confidentiality training, and training in alcohol and HIV risk reduction and medication treatment adherence.

To ensure quality, three levels of supervision and oversight are provided; peer-counselors are supervised by trained social workers; social workers are supervised by a senior social worker; and the senior social workers report to a medical director and are linked to a psychiatric hospital. Peer-counselors receive individual supervision on a regular basis via mobile phone and every three months in person as a group.[37]

This effective task-shifting strategy is allowing the Rwandan Defense Force to scale mental health services to soldiers at high risk of mental problems in ways that increase access and acceptability and maintain quality while lowering costs.

Holding the Key

Noncommunicable diseases pose serious problems throughout the world, regardless of income. However, in developing countries they are more likely to be ignored. Developing countries, however, may hold the key for innovative and low-cost ways that we may be able to tackle them throughout the world.

Community-level care by lower-level community providers is an essential part of care in low-resource settings because it focuses on prevention and low-cost solutions that save lives. These community-level providers may also be the most effective in helping to support the difficult lifestyle changes that are needed to control noncommunicable diseases. Developing countries have also provided innovative models for bringing advanced and specialized treatment to the masses of people who need them through high-quality care that is extremely efficient. Innovative and entrepreneurial solutions for NCDs in developing countries may be a key to many of our problems in global health.

Food for Thought

- What three improvements in efficiency might increase your impact? How might you overcome barriers to test or implement them in the next year?
- List five new ways you could bring in more money or other resources to help you scale up and have more impact.

Part 3
Moving Forward

8

Getting There from Here:
Priorities, Plans, and Progress

The seven-point *IMPACTS* approach provides a framework for saving lives in global health. Frameworks and models, however, don't save lives. People do. It is only when frameworks and models inform the development of plans that guide the actions of people and organizations do we create impacts that change and save lives.

As we've seen throughout this book, the people and organizations that are creating impacts in global health are not acting alone or in isolation. They work in partnership with governments, businesses, NGOs, donors, and others. Though the goals of these various efforts may be very different, such as immunizing children, preventing cervical cancer, or providing affordable care to the poor, they contain common features. They are innovative, entrepreneurial, guided by a plan, and monitored closely. When they hit roadblocks, they find ways around them. When they veer off course, they adjust and get back on track. They are designed to produce impacts.

Many books focus on creating business plans, stimulating innovation and entrepreneurship, managing health systems, and monitoring and evaluation. A number of them are included in the bibliography. Our goal here is to complement those sources with a brief overview of an *IMPACTS*-guided approach to setting priorities, creating plans, and ensuring accountability. Each is an essential component to helping ensure that time and resources are used efficiently and effectively to achieve output, outcomes, and impacts in global health.

On the Road to *IMPACTS*: Planning the Trip

Impact planning requires clarity on priorities both external and internal to the organization. Knowledge of these makes it easier to identify the many opportunities to create impacts in global health that are in alignment with external and internal priorities and needs.

External Priorities and Needs

Numerous challenges with limited resources force governments, communities, and families in developing nations to prioritize multiple competing needs. When roads are impassable, electricity is intermittent, jobs are few, schools are poor, babies are dying, and the government's coffers are bare, everything is a priority. Regardless of whether you are from business, an NGO, or government, there are tremendous challenges in the environment.

All needs are pressing, and health concerns may not be seen as the most critical. There are also priorities within health—AIDS, childhood vaccinations, strokes, cancer, and malaria, among others. The priorities are many, and the resources to meet them are few.

Understanding priorities and needs, as well as the human and financial resources that they are being directed toward, is critical from an *IMPACTS* perspective, because it helps identify opportunities in unmet needs, opportunities to create impacts.

Creating Opportunities: Filling the Gap

In many ways, the larger the gap, the more opportunities may exist for a particularly innovative and entrepreneurial organization to create impact.

When Bangladesh became independent in 1971 it faced substantial challenges not only in health, but in virtually every other sector as well. Many wondered openly whether Bangladesh would survive. Today, though the country remains poor, even in comparison to its relatively poor neighbors—the average income of Pakistan is nearly 50 percent higher and the average income of India is nearly twice as high—it surpasses these countries in terms of life expectancy, maternal and child health indices, and literacy for girls.[1] In the gap between needs and resources in Bangladesh, social innovators and entrepreneurs saw an opportunity to change not only Bangladesh, but the world.

One NGO, BRAC, began as a provider of microloans and basic self-empowered programs to help the poor. However, it has grown into the world's largest NGO serving the poor in terms of the number of people it reaches, 126 million people per year in its microfinance, health, education, and agriculture programs. Innovation is a core pillar of the BRAC approach, so important that this organization, born from a desire to help the poor have better lives, has its own Social Innovation Lab. The lab permits it to test innovative ideas before implementing, disseminating, or scaling them.

Related to the work of BRAC in Bangladesh are the efforts of the Grameen Bank and Muhammad Yunus. Grameen Bank, along with BRAC, helped launch the microfinance movement. Though the movement has not eliminated poverty, it now provides more than $25 billion in microloans to mainly poor but entrepreneurial women throughout the world.[2] In 2006, Grameen Bank and its founder, Muhammad Yunus, won the Nobel Peace Prize for their work related to creating impacts for the poor.

Also in Bangladesh is Smiling Sun, the social franchise network discussed in chapter 5, which provides 25 million people, mostly women and children, with health care each year through its more than 9,000 networked franchise health outlets operated by entrepreneurs. This work is partially supported by self-generated revenue.

Part of the reason that BRAC, an NGO; Grameen, a private bank; and Smiling Sun, a social franchise network, have succeeded is that their work has historically involved a strong, coordinated partnership with government. They were many with the same goal—government, businesses, and NGOs working together to achieve common goals and create global impacts.

Some may see the work that was incubated in the need–resource gap in Bangladesh as an exception to the rule that defines what is possible. We view it, rather, as an example of what can be done when we use innovative and entrepreneurial people to recognize external priorities and then find opportunity in unmet need. This approach has been recognized all over the world, from Bangladesh to Zambia.

When some resources are available to begin to meet needs, there is still a need to prioritize how to do so using *IMPACTS*. In some countries, mainly in Africa, there are now resources to battle HIV/AIDS, an epidemic that only a decade earlier many thought would destroy the continent. However, great impacts are being made today, thanks to PEPFAR, the Global Fund, developing countries, and many others. In these government-led efforts, government ministries generally work with stakeholders—NGOs, businesses, providers, and consumers—to set national priorities, strategies, and targets. Each program is slightly different, since each country's priorities, needs, and resources differ. However, together these innovative programs have helped lead to decreases in new HIV infections, enabled 7 million people in developing countries to get on lifesaving antiretroviral medicines, and saved millions of people throughout the world.

Once external priorities are clear, opportunities for change can be found in the gap of unmet need.

Internal Priorities

Internal priorities are also critical. They determine which of the external priorities are in line with the organization's mission, strategies, and resources. Internal priorities will differ based on the organization and may focus on maternal health, diseases such as HIV, or smoking, and are driven by financial, social, religious, or other reasons, or some combination of them.

Available resources and constraints simply influence *how* opportunities are created rather than whether they *can* be created. Community culture, existing infrastructure, availability of mobile technology, literacy, and preconception of need are all among the factors to be considered when determining what opportunities and which solutions may be most appropriate and most likely to succeed.

Once priorities have been identified, organizations must put an effective plan in place.

Planning the Trip

It is critical for any organization, whether it is a government agency, a business, or an NGO, to have an effective plan if it is to understand where it is, where it wants to go, what the key milestones are, when it is going off course, and when it has reached the destination. We have provided an exercise (see Probes to Create *IMPACTS* Now on page 156) that any program or organization leader can complete to identify the key components of an *IMPACTS* plan. The exercise will help leaders who develop and implement health programs to think about their goals, challenges, and potential opportunities and solutions. We have outlined a number of questions to help managers brainstorm the different *IMPACTS* elements with peers, stakeholders, and partners. These questions are by no means exhaustive; they simply serve as a starting point. The exercise also will serve as a foundation for a business plan and can be used to create a logic model.

These questions were also provided at the end of each chapter in parts 1 and 2. However, as we noted earlier, the most impact occurs in partnerships, so we encourage you to review these questions with your teams, peers, stakeholders, and partners.

There are no right or wrong answers to these questions. Responses will differ based on external and internal circumstances

Probes to Create *IMPACTS* Now

IMPACT Points	Probes
I Innovation & Entrepreneurship	• List three technology or business model innovations that might help your organization increase impact. Whose buy-in might you need to try them?
	• What truly motivates the members of your organization? How might these motivators be incorporated into their work to foster innovative and entrepreneurial thinking and action?
	• Which three peer organizations are the most innovative or entrepreneurial? What do they do differently than you to encourage innovation and entrepreneurship? If you're not sure, how could you find out?
M Maximizing Efficiency & Effectiveness	• What three improvements in efficiency might increase your impact? How might you overcome barriers to test or implement them in the next year?
	• What three things might your organization do to increase the quality of your products or services without increasing costs? How might you overcome barriers to test or implement them in the next year?
	• What safeguards might you put in place to ensure that you don't sacrifice quality for efficiency or vice versa?
P Partner Coordination	• What three organizations might help you achieve greater impact or scale (including government, NGOs, businesses, and donors)? How might you also help them? How might you engage them in this in the next year?
	• What three organizations have access to suppliers, distributors, customers, or champions that might help you achieve greater impact? What might you offer them to help create a win–win partnership?
	• What three organizations in your area have skills that might help you increase impact, for example, in supply chain management, financial controls, training, or marketing? Could they share these skills? What might you offer in return?

A	Accountability	• What are your organization's goals and intended impacts? How do they guide your decisions? How do you share them with others?
		• What metrics are in place to measure your projected outputs, outcomes, and impacts? What milestones have you defined on the road ahead for you and your team?
		• What three things can you do to help team members consistently meet targets for output, outcomes, and impacts?
		• What perspectives might be the most helpful to you as you develop an *IMPACTS* plan for your organization? What people who have those perspectives might you ask to help you? What is your target date for developing your plan?
C	Creating Demand	• What five things might be limiting demand for your products or services? What might you do to overcome these obstacles within the next year?
		• Who might be able to help you create demand for your products or services? How might you engage them in the next year?
		• What might you offer customers to encourage them to bring in new customers?
T	Task Shifting	• Which tasks now performed by highly skilled team members could be handed to others so you could have greater impact? Whose buy-in might you need to help this transition go smoothly?
		• Which tasks might you shift to new settings to help you have greater impact? Whose buy-in might you need to help this transition go smoothly?
		• What might you do to ensure that the quality of shifted tasks remains high (for example, training, supervision, mobile phone applications, checklists, and incentives)? How will you know if you've succeeded?
S	Scaling	• How might you double your impact or the number of people served over the next three years? What obstacles might make this hard? How might you navigate the obstacles?
		• How can you best maintain quality as you expand?
		• List five new ways you could bring in more money or other resources to help you scale up and have more impact.

and the people who are engaged in the process. While we believe it is most helpful to think through all seven points, you may identify one or more as most critical at a particular point in time. If so, focus there and return to the others later.

The questions should inform the development of a business action plan based on your logic model. These plans should be working documents that are reevaluated regularly to ensure that the desired impact is being achieved. Your plan should be clearly laid out, but at the same time it should be flexible enough to allow you to make course corrections.

The Road to *IMPACTS*

The importance of a clear logic model for global health and for individual projects cannot be overemphasized. Field research has consistently documented that many organizations and projects do not have well-developed logic models. We reemphasize this point since a clear definition of success is necessary to ensure accountability. *Pharmacy on a Bicycle* has focused on how to use existing technologies, human and financial capital, systems, and infrastructure to do this. Accountability measures are important not only to determine program success, but as tools for learning how to improve program design and implementation.

The specific logic model designed for each program or project provides the basis for measuring what matters. It must be tailored to individual organizations and the environment in which they operate. A clear logic model should allow you to effectively evaluate success and to identify areas for improvement so you can address them. It provides the elements, including the inputs, processes, outputs, outcomes, and impacts that should be part of the accountability system. The goal is to measure the impacts, but the inputs, processes, outputs, and outcomes are leading indicators of success that also should be measured. The Global Health Impacts Logic Model (Figure 9) presented in Part 1 serves as a visual representation of the relationships among the available resources, needed activities, and desired results.

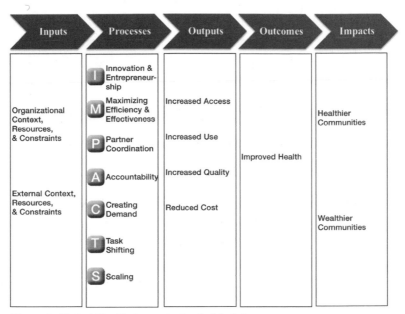

Figure 9 Global Health Impacts Logic Model

The inputs include both the internal environment in which an organization operates and its leadership, management structure and capacity, and the mission guiding its strategic decisions. The organization's internal structures, processes, and systems by which it operates support these and its financial and human resources. Program processes are the internal activities with the given inputs. We recommend using the *IMPACTS* approach for optimal results, which we discussed in detail in Part 1. The outputs in the logic model are the immediate results of the organization's processes. From here, we trace the desired outcomes, which are the specific changes to target populations and communities. Ultimately, this achieves long-term impact, or fundamental changes to communities as a result of the organization's activities. Using a logic model allows organizations to effectively visualize the relationships between activities and evaluate program success.[3]

Driving Success and Ensuring Accountability

Ensuring accountability is a critical element of improving global health. Accountability requires monitoring and evaluating organization activities and determining if you are having the impact you desire. We need to develop clear metrics for measuring progress and providing milestones. Identifying, acknowledging, and communicating both successes and failures are important for reducing illnesses and saving lives. The logic model should guide these activities.

Accountability measures allow your organization to track progress toward its impact goal. They allow you to identify where in the logic model your organization is falling short, enabling corrective action to be specific and targeted. They allow you to identify areas of inefficiency and ineffectiveness, providing visibility into program functions so you can identify what isn't working and what can be done better. Measuring accountability allows you to ensure that all your resources—financial, human, time—are being allocated appropriately.

The logic model provides a critical articulation of what drives success, whereas the metrics indicate to what extent success has been achieved. It is important to measure the impact, but it is also important to measure the inputs, processes, outputs, and outcomes, since these are the leading indicators of success. If the logic model is thought out carefully, each of the elements should be a critical driver of success that culminates in an increase in impact. Further, since measurement of impact is often difficult, measuring these leading indicators may be the best way to evaluate whether your organization is on a path toward success. If some of the leading indicators show weak inputs, processes, outputs, or outcomes, it is likely that you will not achieve the desired impacts.

Developing clear and precise metrics is required on the front end and during the program. Before embarking on the project, we need to assess its feasibility. Can we measure progress? Can we measure successful impact? (See Table 12 for sample metrics.) During the program, we have to be able to monitor progress milestones. This method allows corrective action to be taken early and at multiple junctures during the course of the project. That way, we won't have to wait until we have reached a terminal point before determining that a program did not work.

Table 12 Sample Global Health Metrics

Logic Model Elements	Performance Metrics
Inputs	• Budget allocated to health products and services • Average income of the population • Percent of population more than two hours from health facility • Percent of staff who understand and are aligned with mission • Number of medical personnel per capita • Percent of leadership effectively trained • Percent of health facilities adequately staffed
Processes	• Number of activities task-shifted to lower level providers • Number of activities task-shifted to other settings • Number of new partners engaged • Number of outreach activities to new potential patients • Percent of programs scaled by more than 20 percent • Number of programs scaled by more than 20 percent • Number of new and innovative programs implemented
Outputs	• Number of target population within one mile of services • Number of potential patients reached • Number of potential patients enrolled • Percent of rural poor in program • Cost per patient treated • Number of people educated on issue • Percent of people on appropriate treatment • Percent of patients adhering to treatment
Outcomes	• Number of lost work days • Number of child deaths from disease • Number of incidents of malaria • Percent of complications in deliveries of babies • Average income of participants • Number of programs adopted by other organizations or communities
Impacts	• Average income in community • Percent with disease per 100,000 population • Number who died per 100,000 population

And after the program goals are met, precise metrics allow us to do rigorous internal and external evaluation. This leads to more effective programming in the future, identifies unforeseen outcomes, and demonstrates efficacy that may not be immediately

Table 13 The Difference Between Monitoring and Evaluation

Dimension	Monitoring	Evaluation
Frequency	Periodic, on a regular basis	Episodic, when making strategic decisions
Function	Tracking and oversight	Assessment
Purpose	Improve efficiency, provide information for mid-course corrections to improve outputs and outcomes	Improve effectiveness, impact, value for money, or return on investment; developing strategy, creating policies
Focus	Inputs, processes, operations and outputs	Effectiveness, quality, cost effectiveness, reach, impact
Methods	Routine review of data and report, field observations	Rigorously designed (helps to have outside input); more thorough and intensive
Source of Information	Data summaries (patients reached, seen, treated; products sold; balance sheet and other measures), progress reports, interviews with clients/patients and key stakeholders	Same as for monitoring, as well as local, national or regional data to determine trends and patterns
Cost	Consistent, recurrent	Episodic; generally more expensive than a round of monitoring

Source: Adapted from Global Fund, *Monitoring and Evaluation Toolkit*, 4th ed., November 2011.

visible—such as the fact that fewer infections lead to healthier future populations, which leads to a long-term strengthening of society.

Once a program is developed, it is important to monitor and evaluate your progress. There are important differences between monitoring and evaluation. Monitoring is about measuring progress toward milestones/goals. Monitoring requires clear metrics for measurement. Evaluation, on the other hand, is about measuring impact. The process of effective monitoring is what enables evaluation (Table 13).

Effective performance evaluation and management systems are needed, along with the sharing of information on success and failure. More scaling and replication of existing programs for different geographies, populations, and diseases form a central theme of this book. Program managers need to share successes and failures with others so they can adopt and adapt successful programs in their own environments.

9

Busting Barriers: Heeding the Call

Millions of men, women, and children are dying of diseases we can inexpensively prevent and treat. Now is the time to create impacts in global health and save more lives. Significant technological and business model innovations have been developed that increase access, use, and quality while reducing the cost of health services. For these solutions to save more lives, they must be adapted to new populations and conditions, continually refined, and scaled to reach more people in more regions.

In *Pharmacy on a Bicycle* we have described many innovative and entrepreneurial solutions that have been developed in many countries by governments, NGOs, businesses, and donors to save lives. Fortunately, a confluence of circumstances makes scaling these solutions all the more feasible now. These circumstances include growing economies in many low- and middle-income countries, economic interdependencies among developed countries, investments by developing countries in health, and significant investments by businesses.

We are now at a tipping point to make lasting global health impacts.

Building with More Than BRICS

As the economies of developed countries have struggled, the economies of low- and middle-income countries have soared. Over the past thirty years, the growing economic strength and importance of middle-income countries such as Brazil, Russia, India, China, and South Africa (the BRICS) has been clear.

However, many lower-income countries are also experiencing economic booms. In fact, during the first decade of this century, all of the ten fastest-growing economies were low- and middle-income countries. Between 2011 and 2015 that trend is expected to continue, with the majority being in Africa and the remainder in Asia, and their annual growth is expected to be from 6 percent to 9.5 percent. Together these countries represent over 40 percent of the world population.[1] With economic growth and the development of a middle class, there is more demand for health care and need for health investments, creating the opportunity to build and strengthen the health system.

Economic Interdependencies

The growth of low- and middle-income countries is also fostering economic and political partnerships that expand opportunities for health-related partnerships. We saw in chapter 7 the connections that Narayana Hrudayalaya (NH) has created through telemedicine to train and support doctors in Africa. Relationships like this transfer medical skills and knowledge across national and regional boundaries, enhancing the quality of care for all. These investments by NH benefit everyone as the African health providers receive consultations and training from more experienced doctors at NH, benefitting both the African doctors and their patients. NH then receives referrals of patients from Africa who can afford to pay for care.

In addition, these links promote the flow of ideas and solutions from one place to another, allowing solutions from Honduras to be replicated in Malawi or programs in Pakistan to be modified and implemented in Laos. As innovative and entrepreneurial solutions develop, cross-border relationships can help accelerate global health improvements.

Business Is Good for Health. Health Is Good for Business

Drawn by the growth of these countries and a desire to develop new markets for their products, multinationals are increasingly setting up shop in low- and middle-income countries. IBM, Google, PricewaterhouseCoopers, Nokia/Siemens, Procter & Gamble, and many other companies have recently created regional hubs in Africa. New corporate partners may not only help strengthen the economies of these countries, but may improve health as well.

For example, the IBM Foundation, through the Pink Ribbon Red Ribbon initiative, provided pro bono Corporate Service Corps consultants to develop and recommend a way for the government of Kenya to enhance its data-tracking and screening outreach for cervical cancer. This program helps IBM build closer ties within Kenya, developing important knowledge in the health and infrastructure sectors while gaining a better understanding of the region's business culture. Kenya's health system and its patients may benefit from an enhanced system of care.

But that's not all. IBM invests more than $6 billion in research and development each year, and in 2012 the company opened its first research lab on the African continent in collaboration with the Kenyan government. The investment is intended to advance research in a number of areas, including technologies that can help governments deliver services more effectively and efficiently to citizens.[2] Such investments help to support and stimulate innovators relevant to developing countries. Business is good for health, and health is good for business.

Emerging Leaders

As we've seen through the innovative and entrepreneurial examples presented in *Pharmacy on a Bicycle*, many of the successful solutions that are creating impacts in developing countries are emerging within developing countries themselves, fueled by an emerging group of global health and development leaders. Investments by companies like IBM and others will create additional opportunities for them. Another innovative program, Global Health Corps, was developed to help stimulate and support new cadres of global health leaders in developing countries. Led by Barbara P. Bush, Global Health Corps pairs young leaders from over fifteen countries to work for a year in public and private health-related organizations in Rwanda, Uganda, Malawi, Burundi, and Zambia, as well as in organizations that serve very poor communities in the United States. Due to the high demand for this type of leadership training, they are able to accept less than 2 percent of all the qualified people who apply, making acceptance into Global Health Corps even more competitive than top Ivy League universities.[3]

Another global NGO, Ashoka, seeks to create sustainable change by linking, training, and supporting over 3,000 fellows who work in over sixty countries on innovative and entrepreneurial projects that create social good. Many of these projects focus on health. Organizations such as the Bill and Melinda Gates Foundation and the Skoll Foundation are also encouraging emerging leaders in global health with generous grants to support their innovative and entrepreneurial ideas.

These new emerging leaders and the global health programs they create, from Aravind Eye Centers to the Narayana Hrudayalaya Heart Centers, are important pieces of the puzzle that may not only help us solve health problems in developing countries, but in countries throughout the world.

Putting the Pieces Together

Innovative and entrepreneurial solutions that help make health in many developing countries financially sustainable, along with greater investments in health in low- and middle-income countries, can help put the pieces together to improve access, use, and quality while decreasing cost.

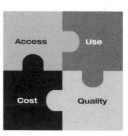

Spheres of Influence

While it has been large corporations and NGOs that have helped influence the global health agenda, all organizations, large and small, can play a role. Each organization, regardless of size or location, has a different sphere of influence. It is important for each to be aware of and appreciate the scope of its actions and operate in a manner that can make the most of its reach. A small organization working within a community has the ability to influence individuals and promote healthy living habits. On the other hand, large multinationals can influence major flows of funding or draw attention to specific health issues.

Although organizations may have a limited sphere of influence, they are able to influence those operating at higher levels to help mold better working environments. For example, an organization operating a network of franchised clinics can nudge government officials to minimize regulatory barriers to allow for task shifting to take place. Governments can reach out to large aid organizations to help spotlight a specific health problem in their country and increase global awareness.

An organization's sphere of influence also includes its internal environment, which determines how it works and functions to accomplish its mission. This internal environment includes an organization's culture, leadership, structure, systems, and resources it has at its disposal. It is important for organizations to build an internal environment that promotes innovative thinking and embraces the entrepreneurial spirit of its workforce.

Leveraging Culture

Health care occurs in a social and cultural context, and to be successful organizations must be consistent with that context, using it to their advantage. To be consistent with social and cultural contexts, we must work with communities and leaders to understand issues, create appropriate programs, and, through a process of mutual respect, instill trust. Cultural differences need not be viewed as an obstacle to achieving success, but rather as providing

Table 14 Key *IMPACTS* Actions

IMPACTS Point	Key Actions
I Innovation & Entrepreneur-ship	• Motivate and reward staff for innovative and entrepre-neurial approaches • Adopt enablers and remove barriers to innovation • Leverage the power of mobile applications to improve data entry, monitoring, provider support, and engage-ment with patients
M Maximizing Efficiency & Effectiveness	• Create efficiencies to make the most out of available resources • Automate services where possible • Verify quality of all products and services, those done directly and those shifted to other providers
P Partner Coor-dination	• Explore partnerships with microenterprises, private com-panies, NGOs, and government entities that could help achieve key objectives
A Account-ability	• Have clear goals, targets, and resources • Evaluate organizational changes on key outputs related to access, use, quality, and costs • Measure outcomes and impacts of organization activity and modify inputs and processes when necessary
C Creating Demand	• Identify and engage champions who can influence change • Provide incentives to create demand • Engage in social awareness campaigns to increase education and awareness
T Task Shifting	• Determine which organizational activities can be task-shifted to lower-level providers and local settings • Identify facilitators of task shifting that can be adopted for existing processes
S Scaling	• Tailor products and services to local cultures • Empower staff to make decisions and take risks

an opportunity to create something new and possibly better. Op-erating in different environments and cultures forces innovative and entrepreneurial thinking and stimulates the creation of ap-propriate solutions. For example, programs distributing white bed nets were unsuccessful in many regions of Africa because they resembled white funeral shrouds. It wasn't until the nets were dyed a different color that use dramatically increased. Cultural diversity should be leveraged to stimulate innovative global health solutions.

Actions for Impact

The IMPACTS approach describes the activities that all organizations can use to significantly improve global health (Table 14). These can lead to improved access, quality, and use while simultaneously reducing cost.

Conclusion

Millions of people around the world from East Timor to South Sudan are dying of diseases we know how to prevent, diagnose, and treat easily and inexpensively. It is not that the science or medical knowledge is lacking. We must do a better job of bringing quality care to those who need it most, in a place that is accessible, in a way that is acceptable, and at a cost that is affordable.

Many organizations are already doing this, in different ways, with different populations, and in different settings. What they have in common is that they are all using innovative and entrepreneurial solutions to solve these problems. In fact, many are disseminating health products and services quite successfully and may not only meet needs in developing countries but may be helpful in all countries, regardless of income.

To be successful they need to be financially sustainable and scaled up. Many can often be easily adapted or adopted to other geographies, settings, diseases, and organizations. This can be done by governments, NGOs, businesses, or partnerships between them.

The IMPACTS approach describes the activities that all organizations can use to significantly improve global health. These can lead to improved access, quality, and use while simultaneously reducing cost. Sometimes this is relatively easy—and sometimes much more difficult because of resource constraints and organizational barriers. But often constraints and barriers can serve to stimulate new solutions that can save lives. The many examples that we have provided here, and the countless more that are in the field, demonstrate the variety of ways that this can be done. The seven-point *IMPACTS* approach provides a guide.

In *Pharmacy on a Bicycle* we have presented an approach to reach those goals. This is not only something that can be done in the future. It is already being done by smart innovators and entrepreneurs in government, NGOs, businesses, and donor groups, large and small. We have discussed how to plan for it, act on it, and monitor your progress toward your goals. We can bring care to people and save lives, regardless of whether it is delivered by a community health worker on foot, by a nurse on a mobile phone, by a medical doctor via telemedicine, or from a pharmacy on a bicycle.

Learn More and Share

Pharmacy on a Bicycle is filled with innovative and entrepreneurial solutions that are creating *IMPACTS* in global health. However, there are many more.

If you have a great program that is creating *IMPACTS* that others should know about, please go to our website, post it, and tell us all about it. We all have much to learn and share.

www.pharmacyonabicycle.com

On the website, you also find loads of additional tips, tools, and exercises for creating *IMPACTS* in global health.

Notes

Notes to the Introduction

1. Based upon accounts provided in *A Relay Race to Save Lives During Bandhs*, posted by Fungma Fudong and the Saath-Saath Project staff on Thursday, August 30, 2012, http://blog.usaid.gov/2012/08/a-relay-race-to-save-lives-during-bandhs/. Names have been changed and dialogue is fictitious; otherwise, the events occurred as reported.

2. For the purposes of this book, we have classified countries into low-, middle-, and high-income countries. This classification is based on the World Bank's definitions using 2011 gross national income (GNI) per capita. Low-income countries are those with GNI per capita less than $1,026. We have combined the lower- and upper-middle income groups defined by the World Bank into a single middle-income group. These countries have a GNI per capita between $1,026 and $12,475. High-income countries are those with GNI greater than $12,475. When we use the term *developing countries*, we are referring to low- and middle-income countries. Although we have classified countries into these large groups, we realize that every country, whether classified as upper-, middle-, or lower-income, will have subpopulations that are wealthy, middle-income, and poor.

Notes to Chapter 1

1. Wang et al. (2012) "Age-Specific and Sex-Specific Mortality in 187 Countries, 1970–2010: A Systematic Analysis for the Global Burden of Disease Study 2010"; Lozano et al. (2012) "Global and Regional Mortality from 235 Causes of Death

for 20 Age Groups in 1990 and 2010: A Systematic Analysis for the Global Burden of Disease Study 2010."

2. Wang et al. (2012) "Age-Specific and Sex-Specific Mortality in 187 Countries, 1970–2010"; World Health Organization (2009) *Investing in Maternal, Newborn, and Child Health: The Case for Asia and the Pacific.*

3. Haskell (2003) "Cardiovascular Disease Prevention and Lifestyle Interventions: Effectiveness and Efficacy"; World Health Organization (2012) "Cardiovascular Diseases (CVDs) Fact Sheet"; Mayne (2001) "Nutrient Intake and Risk of Subtypes of Esophageal and Gastric Cancer"; Rothwell et al. (2012) "Effect of Daily Aspirin on Risk of Cancer Metastasis: A Study of Incident Cancers During Randomised Controlled Trials"; Rothwell et al. (2012) "Short-Term Effects of Daily Aspirin on Cancer Incidence, Mortality, and Non-Vascular Death: Analysis of the Time Course of Risks and Benefits in 51 Randomised Controlled Trials"; Raju et al. (2011) "Effect of Aspirin on Mortality in the Primary Prevention of Cardiovascular Disease."

4. Sankaranarayanan et al. (2007) "Effect of Visual Screening on Cervical Cancer Incidence and Mortality in Tamil Nadu, India: A Cluster-Randomised Trial."

5. Dandona et al. (2002) "Refractive Error in Children in a Rural Population in India."

6. Patel et al. (2011) "Lay Health Worker Led Intervention for Depressive and Anxiety Disorders in India: Impact on Clinical and Disability Outcomes over 12 Months."

7. Wang et al. (2012) "Age-Specific and Sex-Specific Mortality in 187 Countries, 1970–2010"; Lozano et al. (2012) "Global and Regional Mortality from 235 Causes of Death for 20 Age Groups in 1990 and 2010."

8. World Health Organization, United Nations Children's Fund, and Joint United Nations Programme on HIV/AIDS (2011) *Global HIV/AIDS Response: Progress Report 2011*; World Health Organization (2012) "HIV/AIDS Fact Sheet."

9. Similar initiatives to reduce malaria deaths such as the President's Malaria Initiative and Malaria No More improve health outcomes related to development such as the ONE Campaign, and multiple other initiatives and international bodies, such as the World Health Organization, United Nations–affiliated bodies, the Clinton Global Initiative, and the GAVI Alliance (formerly the Global Alliance for Vaccines and Immunisations), among others, have also greatly helped. Improvements in maternal and child health have been supported by many organizations that have worked together, such as GAVI, UNICEF, CIFF (Children's Investment Ford Foundation), and the Gates Foundation. Investments are coming not just from foreign entities but local governments. Domestic HIV investments by low- and middle-

income countries reached US$8.6 billion in 2011—the highest amount ever; Dunham (2008) "Bush Signs Expansion of Global AIDS Programs"; United Nations Development Programme (2011) *Towards Human Resilience: Sustaining MDG Progress in an Age of Economic Uncertainty.*

10. Zambrano and Seward (2012) *Mobile Technologies and Empowerment: Enhancing Human Development through Participation and Innovation;* Zuckerman (2009) "Web 2.0 Tools for Development: Simple Tools for Smart People."

11. Connor, Rafter, and Rodgers (2004) "Do Fixed-Dose Combination Pills or Unit-of-Use Packaging Improve Adherence? A Systematic Review."

12. Dybul, Piot, and Frenk (2012) "Reshaping Global Health."

13. Leach-Kemon et al. (2012) "The Global Financial Crisis Has Led to a Slowdown in Growth of Funding to Improve Health in Many Developing Countries"; Institute for Health Metrics and Evaluation (2011) *Financing Global Health 2011: Continued Growth as MDG Deadline Approaches.*

14. Mehta and Shenoy (2011) *Infinite Vision: How Aravind Became the World's Greatest Business Case for Compassion;* Vickers (2011) *Driving Down the Cost of High-Quality Care: Lessons from the Aravind Eye Care System.*

15. International Finance Corporation (2007) *The Business of Health in Africa: Partnering with the Private Sector to Improve People's Health.*

16. VisionSpring (2012) "What We Do."

17. Chuma et al. (2010) "Towards Achieving Abuja Targets: Identifying and Addressing Barriers to Access and Use of Insecticides Treated Nets Among the Poorest Populations in Kenya."

18. Mugeni, Ngabo, and Humuza (2012) "Community Performance–Based Financing in Health: Incentivizing Mothers and Community Health Workers to Improve Maternal Health Outcomes in Rwanda."

19. Fairall et al. (2012) "Task Shifting of Antiretroviral Treatment from Doctors to Primary-Care Nurses in South Africa (STRETCH): A Pragmatic, Parallel, Cluster-Randomised Trial."

20. Wakabi (2008) "Extension Workers Drive Ethiopia's Primary Health Care."

21. UNICEF (2012) "Innovations: Uganda."

22. Ibid.

23. Prata et al. (2011) "Provision of Injectable Contraceptives in Ethiopia Through Community-Based Reproductive Health Agents"; Chibanda et al. (2011) "Problem-Solving Therapy for Depression and Common Mental Disorders in Zimbabwe: Piloting a Task-Shifting Primary Mental Health Care Intervention in a Population with a High Prevalence of People Living with HIV."

24. W.K. Kellogg Foundation (2004) *Logic Model Development Guide.* The internal culture is important and defines how an organization operates on a day-to-

day basis. Leadership helps develop and maintain the culture, but it is also impacted by the organizational strategy and structure. These components can either create or break down barriers to communication, as well as define the latitude within which employees have to operate. The resource constraints of an organization are also important factors. Both financial and talent resources must be accounted for in order to meet the objectives of an organization. Financial resources are needed to get off the ground and operate, while human resources are needed to run programs and solve problems.

Notes to Chapter 2

1. Williams (2012) "Rice's Student-Designed Device to Help Babies Breathe Wins More Support."
2. Brown et al. (2011) "A Hand-Powered, Portable, Low-Cost Centrifuge for Diagnosing Anemia in Low-Resource Settings."
3. PATH (2012) *Annual Report 2011.*
4. Byrne and Gerdes (2005) "The Man Who Invented Management: Why Peter Drucker's Ideas Still Matter"; Drucker (2002) "The Discipline of Innovation."
5. Davila, Epstein, and Shelton (2013) "Making Innovation Work: How to Manage It, Measure It, and Profit from It."
6. The academic literature focuses mostly on technological innovations: Henderson and Clark (1990) "Architectural Innovation: The Reconfiguration of Existing Product Technologies and the Failure of Established Firms"; Christensen and Rosenbloom (1995) "Explaining the Attacker's Advantage: Technological Paradigms, Organizational Dynamics and the Value Network"; and Abernathy and Utterback (1978) "Patterns of Industrial Innovation."
7. Some authors have also included the market as an additional dimension to technology to understand innovation (for example, Afuah, *Innovation Management* [1998]). We believe that focusing on the market unnecessarily restricts the locus of innovation to one piece of the business model.
8. Much of the content in this chapter is drawn from Davila, Epstein, and Shelton (2013) *Making Innovation Work: How to Manage It, Measure It, and Profit from It.*
9. For the importance of process change, see Pisano (1997) *The Development Factory: Unlocking the Potential of Process Innovation.*
10. Examples of process improvements are numerous around the quality movement—for example, Cole (1998) "Learning from the Quality Movement: What Did and Didn't Happen and Why?"; and Juran (1992) *Juran on Quality*

by Design: The New Steps for Planning Quality into Goods and Services.

11. Davila, Epstein, and Shelton (2013) *Making Innovation Work.*

12. For this model, see Tushman and Anderson (1986) "Technological Discontinuities and Organizational Environment."

13. The idea of incremental innovation has been applied to the technology innovation dimension; see Dewar and Dutton (1986) "The Adoption of Radical and Incremental Innovations: An Empirical Analysis"; Ettlie, Bridges, and O'Keefe (1984) "Organizational Strategy and Structural Differences for Radical versus Incremental Innovation"; and Green, Gavin, and Aiman-Smith (1995) "Assessing a Multidimensional Measure of Radical Innovation."

14. Incremental innovation is critical to sustain a firm's position in the market. See Banbury and Mitchell (1995) "The Effect of Introducing Important Incremental Innovations on Market Share and Business Survival."

15. Spector et al. (2012) "Improving Quality of Care for Maternal and Newborn Health: Prospective Pilot Study of the WHO Safe Childbirth Checklist Program."

16. Semi-radical innovation is a common way to break away from incremental innovation but still rely on a subset of core competencies (Utterback (1994) *Mastering the Dynamics of Innovation: How Companies Can Seize Opportunities in the Face of Technological Change.*

17. Pop-Eleches et al. (2011) "Mobile Phone Technologies Improve Adherence to Antiretroviral Treatment in a Resource-Limited Setting: A Randomized Controlled Trial of Text Message Reminders."

18. Global Health Group and University of California, San Francisco (2012) *Clinical Social Franchising Compendium: An Annual Survey of Programs.*

19. See Cooper and Smith (1992) "How Established Firms Respond to Threatening Technologies"; Damanpour (1996) "Organizational Complexity and Innovation: Developing and Testing Contingency Models"; and Foster (1986) *Innovation: The Attacker's Advantage.* For the high level of unsuccessful radical innovations, see Dougherty and Hardy (1996) "Sustained Product Innovation in Large, Mature Organizations: Overcoming Innovation-to-Organization Problems."

20. Radical innovation typically comes from architectural changes (Henderson and Clark [1990] "Architectural Innovation: The Reconfiguration of Existing Product Technologies and the Failure of Established Firms"; Baldwin and Clark [2000] *Design Rules: The Power of Modularity)*; and destroys current competencies (Anderson and Tushman [1990] "Technological Discontinuities and Dominant Designs: A Cyclical Model of Technological Change"; Tushman and Anderson [1986] "Technological Discontinuities and Organizational Environment"; and Tushman and Murmann [1998] "Dominant

Designs, Technology Cycles, and Organizational Outcomes").

21. These game changers have also been called *technological discontinuities* (Ehrenberg [1995] "On the Definition and Measurement of Technological Discontinuities."

22. Bhattacharyya (2010) "Innovative Health Service Delivery Models in Low- and Middle-Income Countries: What Can We Learn from the Private Sector?"; Macke, Misra, and Sharma (2003) "Jaipur Foot: Challenging Convention"; Kanani (2011) "Jaipur Foot: One of the Most Technologically Advanced Social Enterprises in the World"; personal communication with D.R. Mehta, Founder and Chief Patron, BMVSS, December 18, 2012.

23. Radical innovation is frequently associated with startup companies that upset the current industry structure. For the problems facing incumbents when threatened by an external radical innovation, see Day and Schoemaker (2000) "Avoiding the Pitfalls of Emerging Technologies."

24. Radical innovation also has a larger probability of being born in the interfaces of current business units requiring the participation of these various units—a concept called *white spaces* (Hamel and Prahalad [1994] *Competing for the Future*)—with a significant chance of shifting the current strategy. The need for resources from various units and the strategic disruptive nature are labeled as the "scope" and "reach" of the innovation (Burgelman and Doz (2001) "The Power of Strategic Integration").

25. See Radjou, Prabhu, and Ahuja (2012) *Jugaad Innovation: Think Frugal, Be Flexible, Generate Breakthrough Growth*; Sehgal, Dehoff, and Panneer (2010) *The Importance of Frugal Engineering*.

26. See Govindarajan and Trimble (2012) *Reverse Innovation: Create Far from Home, Win Everywhere*; and Immelt, Govindarajan, and Trimble (2009) *How GE Is Disrupting Itself*.

27. Govindarajan and Trimble (2012) *Reverse Innovation*.

28. Stevenson (1983) "A Perspective on Entrepreneurship."

29. Stevenson (2000) "Why Entrepreneurship Has Won!"

30. United Nations Industrial Development Organization (2008) "Creating an Enabling Environment for Private Sector Development in Sub-Saharan Africa."

31. Parker (2006) *The Life Cycle of Entrepreneurial Ventures*.

32. Chen and Ravallion (2010) "The Developing World Is Poorer Than We Thought, But No Less Successful in the Fight against Poverty."

33. Consultative Group to Assist the Poor (2011) *Advancing Financial Access for the World's Poor: Annual Report 2011*.

34. De Mel, McKenzie, and Woodruff (2008) "Returns to Capital in Microenterprises: Evidence from a Field Experiment."

35. Hammond et al. (2007) *The Next 4 Billion: Market Size and Business Strategy at the Base of the Pyramid.*

36. Prahalad (2010) *Fortune at the Bottom of the Pyramid: Eradicating Poverty Through Profits.*

37. Wakabi (2008) "Extension Workers Drive Ethiopia's Primary Health Care"; Bilal et al. (2011) "Health Extension Workers in Ethiopia: Improved Access and Coverage for the Rural Poor."

38. VisionSpring (2012) "What We Do."

39. Katayama (2010) "How Health Care Nonprofit Living Goods Learned a Lesson from Avon Ladies."

40. Fertig and Tzaras (2005) *What Works: Heathstore's Franchise Approach to Healthcare.*

41. Ibid.; Berk and Adhvaryu (2012) "The Impact of a Novel Franchise Clinic Network on Access to Medicines and Vaccinations in Kenya: A Cross-Sectional Study"; personal communication with Greg Starbird, CEO, The HealthStore Foundation, December 20, 2012.

Notes to Chapter 3

1. Ranson et al. (2010) "Priorities for Research into Human Resources for Health in Low- and Middle-Income Countries."

2. World Health Organization (2011) *mHealth: New Horizons for Health Through Mobile Technologies.*

3. E Health Point (2012) "E Health Point"; personal communication with Ashok Mehta, Head, HR & Administration, HealthPoint Services India, January 1, 2013.

4. Riders for Health, "Our Impact."

5. World Bicycle Relief (2007) *Impact of Bicycle Distribution on Tsunami Recovery in Sri Lanka, Final Report.*

6. World Bicycle Relief, *Impact;* Personal communication with Dave Neiswander, Africa Director, World Bicycle Relief, December 13, 2012.

7. Bicycling Empowerment Network (BEN) Nambia, "Strengthening the Grassroots Response to HIV/AIDS."

8. Riders for Health, "Our Approach."

9. AID Village Clinics is no longer in operation; AID Village Clinics, "Africa Infectious Disease Village Clinics: Our Mission"; personal communication with Ann Lurie, Founder AID Village Clinics, Inc., December 13, 2012.

10. Spector et al. (2012) "Improving Quality of Care for Maternal and Newborn Health: Prospective Pilot Study of the WHO Safe Childbirth Checklist Program."

11. World Health Organization and World Alliance for Patient Safety (2008)

Implementation Manual Surgical Safety Checklist: Safe Surgery Saves Lives.

12. Haynes et al. (2009) "A Surgical Safety Checklist to Reduce Morbidity and Mortality in a Global Population."

13. World Health Organization (2012) "Family Planning Fact Sheet."

14. Prata et al. (2008) "Saving Maternal Lives in Resource-Poor Settings: Facing Reality."

15. UNICEF (2010) *Facts for Life.*

16. Roberts et al. (2001) "Keeping Clean Water in a Malawi Refugee Camp: A Randomized Intervention Trial."

17. Choi et al. (1995) "The Effectiveness of Insecticide-Impregnated Bed Nets in Reducing Cases of Malaria Infection: A Meta-Analysis of Published Results."

18. Haskell (2003) "Cardiovascular Disease Prevention and Lifestyle Interventions: Effectiveness and Efficacy"; Mayne (2001) "Nutrient Intake and Risk of Subtypes of Esophageal and Gastric Cancer"; Rothwell et al. (2012) "Effect of Daily Aspirin on Risk of Cancer Metastasis"; Rothwell et al. (2012) "Short-Term Effects of Daily Aspirin on Cancer Incidence, Mortality, and Non-Vascular Death"; Raju et al. (2011) "Effect of Aspirin on Mortality in the Primary Prevention of Cardiovascular Disease."

19. Sweat et al. (2012) "Effects of Condom Social Marketing on Condom Use in Developing Countries: A Systematic Review and Meta-Analysis, 1990–2010."

20. Bertrand et al. (2011) "Voluntary Medical Male Circumcision: A Qualitative Study Exploring the Challenges of Costing Demand Creation in Eastern and Southern Africa."

21. World Health Organization (2012) "Voluntary Medical Male Circumcision for HIV Prevention."

22. Kenya National Bureau of Statistics, ICF Macro (2010) *Kenya Demographic and Health Survey 2008–09.*

23. Kenya National Bureau of Statistics, ICF Macro (2010) *Kenya Demographic and Health Survey 2008–09;* Kenya Ministry of Health National AIDS and STI Control Programme (2009) *Kenya AIDS Indicator Survey 2007 Final Report.*

24. Mwandi et al. (2011) "Voluntary Medical Male Circumcision: Translating Research into the Rapid Expansion of Services in Kenya, 2008–2011."

25. Jokhio, Winter, and Cheng (2005) "An Intervention Involving Traditional Birth Attendants and Perinatal and Maternal Mortality in Pakistan."

26. This data was obtained from Figure 2 of Lozano et al. (2012) "Global and Regional Mortality from 235 Causes of Death for 20 Age Groups in 1990 and 2010"; World Health Organization (2006) *Oral Rehydration Salts: Production of the New ORS*; Munos, Walker, and Black (2010) "The Effect of

Oral Rehydration Solution and Recommended Home Fluids on Diarrhoea Mortality."

27. Beverage Industry (2011) "Sports Drink Sales Get into Shape."

28. World Health Organization (2006) *Stop The Global Epidemic of Chronic Disease: A Practical Guide to Successful Advocacy*.

29. Ibid.

30. Teklehaimanot, Sachs, and Curtis (2007) "Malaria Control Needs Mass Distribution of Insecticidal Bednets"; Curtis et al. (2003) "Scaling-Up Coverage with Insecticide-Treated Nets Against Malaria in Africa: Who Should Pay?"

31. Khatib (2008) "Markets, Voucher Subsidies and Free Nets Combine to Achieve High Bed Net Coverage in Rural Tanzania."

32. Ibid.

33. Bellows, Bellows, and Warren (2011) "Systematic Review: The Use of Vouchers for Reproductive Health Services in Developing Countries: Systematic Review."

34. Meuwissen et al. (2006) "Does a Competitive Voucher Program for Adolescents Improve the Quality of Reproductive Health Care? A Simulated Patient Study in Nicaragua."

35. Ekirapa-Kiracho (2011) "Increasing Access to Institutional Deliveries Using Demand and Supply Side Incentives: Early Results from a Quasi-Experimental Study: An Innovative Approach to Building Capacity at an African University to Improve Health Outcomes."

36. Ahmed and Khan (2011) "Is Demand-Side Financing Equity Enhancing? Lessons from a Maternal Health Voucher Scheme in Bangladesh."

37. Iqbal (2009) "Reaching the Poor with Performance-Based Payment for Safe Delivery Services in Rural Bangladesh: Potential of Performance-Based Payment."

38. United Nations (2011) *The Millennium Development Goals Report 2011*.

Notes to Chapter 4

1. Mangham and Hanson (2010) "Scaling Up in International Health: What Are the Key Issues?"

2. Samoff, Sebatane, and Dembélé (2001) "Scaling Up by Focusing Down: Creating Space to Expand Education Reform."

3. Epstein and Yuthas (2012) "Scaling Effective Education for the Poor in Developing Countries: A Report from the Field."

4. Clark et al. (2012) "Scaling Social Impact: A Literature Toolkit for Funders."

5. Bradach (2003) "Going to Scale: The Challenge of Replicating Social Programs."

6. La France et al. (2006) *Scaling Capacities: Supports for Growing Impact*.

7. Bradach (2003) "Going to Scale"; Crutchfield and McLeod (2007) "Forces for Good: The Six Practices of High-Impact Nonprofits."

8. Dees, Anderson, and Wei-Skillern (2004) "Scaling Social Impact: Strategies for Spreading Social Innovation."

9. Crutchfield and McLeod (2007) "Forces for Good"; Bloom and Dees (2008) "Cultivate Your Ecosystem."

10. Epstein and Yuthas (2012) "Scaling Effective Education for the Poor in Developing Countries."

11. This section relies heavily on Epstein and Yuthas (2012) "Scaling Effective Education for the Poor in Developing Countries."

12. Care International (2011) *Annual Report 2011*.

13. Colclough (1998) "Marketizing Education and Health in Developing Countries: Miracle or Mirage?"

14. Oxfam (2001) "Education: Tackling the Global Crisis."

15. Epstein and Yuthas (2012) "Scaling Effective Education for the Poor in Developing Countries."

16. Chib (2008) *Information and Communication Technologies for Health Care: Midwife Mobile-Phone Project in Aceh Besar*.

17. Glennan et al. (2004) "Expanding the Reach of Education Reforms: Perspectives from Leaders in the Scale-Up of Educational Interventions."

18. Chimombo (2005) "Quantity Versus Quality in Education: Case Studies in Malawi."

19. Ritzer (1993) "The McDonaldization of Society"; Chimombo (2005) "Quantity Versus Quality in Education: Case Studies in Malawi."

20. Epstein and Yuthas (2012) "Scaling Effective Education for the Poor in Developing Countries."

21. Quint et al. (2005) *The Challenge of Scaling Up Educational Reform: Findings and Lessons from First Things First*; Cooper, Slavin, and Madden (1998) "Success for All: Improving the Quality of Implementation of Whole-School Change through the Use of a National Reform Network"; Epstein and Yuthas (2012) "Scaling Effective Education for the Poor in Developing Countries."

22. Kantamara, Hallinger, and Jatiket (2006) "Scaling-Up Education Reform in Thailand: Context, Collaboration, Networks, and Change"; Fullen (2007) "The New Meaning of Education Change."

23. Fullan (2000) "The Return of Large-Scale Reform"; Fullan (2009) "The Role of Leadership in the Promotion of Knowledge Management in Schools."

24. Epstein and Yuthas (2012) "Scaling Effective Education for the Poor in Developing Countries"; Elmore (1996) "Getting to Scale with Good Educational Practice."

25. Commonwealth Secretariat (2005) *Promising Practices and Implications for*

Scaling Up Girls' Education; Samoff, Sebatane, and Dembélé (2001) "Scaling Up by Focusing Down: Creating Space to Expand Education Reform."

26. Bodilly and Augustine (2008) "Revitalizing Arts Education Through Community-Wide Coordination"; Kirby, Berends, and Naftel (2001) "Implementation in a Longitudinal Sample of New American Schools: Four Years into Scale-Up."

27. Glennan et al. (2004) "Expanding the Reach of Education Reforms: Perspectives from Leaders in the Scale-Up of Educational Interventions"; Datnow, Hubbard, and Mehan (2002) "Extending Educational Reform: From One School to Many."

28. BRAC Communication (2012) "Stay Informed: BRAC at a Glance"; personal communication with Scott MacMillan, Communications Manager, BRAC USA, December 13, 2012.

29. Bloom and Chatterji (2009) "Scaling Social Entrepreneurial Impact."

30. Epstein and Yuthas (2012) "Scaling Effective Education for the Poor in Developing Countries."

31. Ibid.

32. Reich (2000) *Public-Private Partnerships for Public Health*; Nishtar (2004) "Public-Private 'Partnerships' in Health: A Global Call to Action."

33. Ibid.; Atun et al. (2012) "Innovative Financing for Health: What Is Truly Innovative?"

34. GAVI Alliance (2011) "Progress Report 2011"; GAVI Alliance (2012) "GAVI's Impact: Saving Lives."

35. Fertig and Tzaras (2005) *What Works: HealthStore's Franchise Approach to Healthcare.*

36. Lehr (2008) *Microfranchising at the Base of the Pyramid.*

37. Ibid.

38. Sireau (2011) *Microfranchising: How Entrepreneurs Are Building a New Road to Development.*

39. Fertig and Tzaras (2007) "Franchising Health Care for Kenya: The HealthStore Foundation Model"; Fairbourne, Gibson, and Gibb Dyer Jr. (2008) *MicroFranchising: Creating Wealth at the Bottom of the Pyramid.*

Notes to Chapter 5

1. Lozano et al. (2012) "Global and Regional Mortality from 235 Causes of Death for 20 Age Groups in 1990 and 2010: A Systematic Analysis for the Global Burden of Disease Study 2010."

2. Ibid.

3. We recognize that men also play important roles in child rearing. However,

globally, particularly in developing countries, this role is almost always as-
sumed by a woman; Dybul (2012) "Finding Common Ground to Save the
Lives of Women and Children and Create Happy, Healthy Families."

4. WHO (2010) *Maternal Health: Investing in the Lifeline of Healthy Societies &
Economies*; UNICEF (2007) *The State of the World's Children 2007.*

5. Quisumbing, Haddad, and Peña (2001) "Are Women Overrepresented
among the Poor? An Analysis of Poverty in Ten Developing Countries";
WHO (2010) *Maternal Health: Investing in the Lifeline of Healthy Societies &
Economies.*

6. Wang et al. (2012) "Age-Specific and Sex-Specific Mortality in 187 Countries,
1970–2010"; Lozano et al. (2012) "Global and Regional Mortality from 235
Causes of Death for 20 Age Groups in 1990 and 2010."

7. Guttmacher Institute (2002) "Family Planning Can Reduce High Infant
Mortality Levels."

8. Setty-Venugopal and Upadhyay (2002) "Birth Spacing: Three to Five Saves
Lives"; Rutstein (2005) "Effects of Preceding Birth Intervals on Neonatal,
Infant and Under-Five Years Mortality and Nutritional Status in Developing
Countries: Evidence from the Demographic and Health Surveys."

9. Trussell (2011) *Contraceptive Efficacy.*

10. Singh and Darroch (2012) *Adding it Up: Costs and Benefits of Contraceptive
Services: Estimates for 2012*; Creanga et al. (2011) "Low Use of Contraception
among Poor Women in Africa: An Equity Issue."

11. Sedgh et al. (2012) "Induced Abortion: Incidence and Trends Worldwide
from 1995 to 2008."

12. WHO (2010) *Countdown to 2015: Maternal, Newborn, and Child Survival.*

13. UNICEF (2007) *The State of the World's Children 2007.*

14. Prata et al. (2012) "New Hope: Community-Based Misoprostol Use to Prevent Postpartum Haemorrhage."

15. Wang et al. (2012) "Age-Specific and Sex-Specific Mortality in 187 Countries,
1970–2010: A Systematic Analysis for the Global Burden of Disease Study
2010"; Lozano et al. (2012) "Global and Regional Mortality from 235 Causes
of Death for 20 Age Groups in 1990 and 2010"; World Health Organization
(2012) "Children: Reducing Mortality Fact Sheet."

16. WHO (2005) *World Health Report 2005: Make Every Mother and Child Count.*

17. UNICEF (2012) *The State of the World's Children 2012.*

18. This data was obtained from Figure 2, Lozano et al. (2012) "Global and
Regional Mortality from 235 Causes of Death for 20 Age Groups in 1990
and 2010."

19. UNICEF and WHO (2009) *Diarrhoea: Why Children Are Still Dying and What
Can Be Done*; WHO (2009) "More Research Needed into Childhood Diarrhea."

20. Sobsey et al. (2008) "Point-of-Use Household Drinking Water Filtration: A Practical, Effective Solution for Providing Sustained Access to Safe Drinking Water in the Developing World"; Hoffman (2009) "Lifestraw Saves Those without Access to Clean Drinking Water." Other water purification systems include P&G's Pur, Unilever's Pureit, and Tata's Swach, which are simply filters that clean the water that is passed through them.

21. Economist (2010) "First Break All the Rules: The Charms of Frugal Innovation."

22. General Electric (2010) *Healthymagination 2010 Annual Report*.

23. Coca-Cola (2012) "Partnership with DEKA R&D to Help Bring Clean Water to Communities in Need"; personal communication with Derk Hendriksen, General Manager, Coca-Cola Company DEKA Project, December 18, 2012.

24. WHO, UNICEF, and World Bank (2009) *State of the World's Vaccines and Immunization*.

25. Ibid.

26. GAVI (2010) *GAVI Alliance Progress Report 2010*.

27. Ibid.

28. WHO, UNICEF, and World Bank (2009) *State of the World's Vaccines and Immunization*.

29. Frontline Health Workers Coalition (2012) "Frontline Health Workers: The Best Way to Save Lives, Accelerate Progress on Global Health, and Help Advance U.S. Interests."

30. WHO (2009) *Monitoring Emergency Obstetric Care: A Handbook*.

31. Prata et al. (2012) "Training Traditional Birth Attendants to Use Misoprostol and an Absorbent Delivery Mat in Home Births."

32. UNDP (2011) *Human Development Report 2011: Sustainability and Equality, A Better Future for All*.

33. Central Statistical Agency of Ethiopia (2012) *Ethiopia Demographic and Health Survey 2011*.

34. Central Statistical Agency of Ethiopia (2001) *Ethiopia Demographic and Health Survey 2000*; El-Saharty et al. (2009) *Ethiopia: Improving Health Service Delivery*.

35. Central Statistical Agency of Ethiopia (2012) *Ethiopia Demographic and Health Survey 2011*.

36. Health Logistics Quarterly (2011) "USAID Deliver Project Provides Technical Assistance to the Pharmaceutical Fund and Supply Agency (PFSA)."

37. Bilal et al. (2011) "Health Extension Workers in Ethiopia: Improved Access and Coverage for the Rural Poor"; Ramundo (2012) "The Female 'Army' Leading Ethiopia's Health Revolution"; personal communication with John Kraemer, Assistant Professor, Georgetown School of Nursing and Health Studies, December 16, 2012.

38. Verpoorten (2005) "The Death Toll of the Rwandan Genocide: A Detailed Analysis for Gikongoro Province."

39. United Nations Populations Fund Rwanda (2011) *Maternal Mortality Reduction Programme in Rwanda*; WHO, UNICEF, and UNFPA (2004) *Maternal Mortality in 2000*.

40. United Nations Populations Fund Rwanda (2011) *Maternal Mortality Reduction Programme in Rwanda*.

41. Holmes (2010) "Rwanda: An Injection of Hope."

42. National Institute of Statistics of Rwanda (2007) *Millennium Development Goals Country Report 2007*.

43. Mugeni, Ngabo, and Humuza (2011) "Community Performance-Based Financing in Health: Incentivizing Mothers and Community Health Workers to Improve Maternal Health Outcomes in Rwanda."

44. Joint Learning Network for Universal Health Coverage, "Rwanda: Mutuelles de Santé."

45. Gertler and Vermeersch (2012) *Using Performance Incentives to Improve Health Outcomes*.

46. Ibid.

47. WHO (2012) *Classifying Health Workers: Mapping Occupations to the International Standard Classification*.

48. Makokha (2011) "Kenya: State Bans Traditional Birth Attendants in Matungu."

49. Masina (2011) "Debate Rages Over Traditional Birth Assistants U-Turn in Malawi"; Prata et al. (2012) "Training Traditional Birth Attendants to Use Misoprostol and an Absorbant Delivery Mat in Home Births"; Wilson et al. (2011) "Effectiveness of Strategies Incorporating Training and Support of Traditional Birth Attendants on Perinatal and Maternal Mortality: Meta-Analysis."

50. Byrne and Morgan (2011) "How the Integration of Traditional Birth Attendants with Formal Health Systems Can Increase Skilled Birth Attendance."

51. Zafar Ullah et al. (2006) "Government–NGO Collaboration: The Case of Tuberculosis in Bangladesh."

52. Despite the high rates of maternal mortality in Bangladesh, rates have decreased from 400 per 100,000 live births in 2000 to 240 in 2010; World Health Organization (2012) *World Health Statistics 2012*.

53. The Global Health Group (2011) *Clinical Social Franchising Case Study Series: Smiling Sun Franchise Program Bangladesh*; Rannan-Eliya (2010) *Bangladesh National Health Accounts, 1997–2007*; World Bank (2004) *Private Sector Assessment for Health, Nutrition and Population (HNP) in Bangladesh*.

54. The Global Health Group (2011) *Clinical Social Franchising Case Study Series:*

Smiling Sun Franchise Program Bangladesh; World Bank (2004) *Private Sector Assessment for Health, Nutrition and Population (HNP) in Bangladesh.*

55. The Global Health Group (2011) *Clinical Social Franchising Case Study Series: Smiling Sun Franchise Program Bangladesh.*

56. The Global Health Group (2012) *Clinical Social Franchising Compendium.*

57. The Global Health Group (2011) *Clinical Social Franchising Case Study Series: Smiling Sun Franchise Program Bangladesh.*

58. Ibid.

59. Health Keepers was developed by Freedom From Hunger.

60. Health Unbound, "MAMA: Mobile Alliance for Maternal Action"; Baby-Center, "Mobile Health."

61. Ibid.

62. General Electric (2010) *Healthymagination 2010 Annual Report.*

Notes to Chapter 6

1. Lozano et al. (2012) "Global and Regional Mortality from 235 Causes of Death for 20 Age Groups in 1990 and 2010"; Globocan (2008) "Cervical Cancer Incidence, Mortality, and Prevalence Worldwide in 2008."

2. Sellors and Sankaranarayanan (2003) "Treatment of cervical intraepithelial neoplasia by cryotherapy."

3. Baseman and Koutsky (2005) "The Epidemiology of Human Papillomavirus Infections."

4. Kitchener, Castle, and Cox (2006) "Achievements and Limitations of Cervical Cytology Screening"; Kreiss et al. (1992) "Human Immunodeficiency Virus, Human Papillomavirus, and Cervical Intraepithelian Neoplasia in Nairobi Prostitutes."

5. Sellors and Sankaranarayanan (2003) "Treatment of cervical intraepithelial neoplasia by cryotherapy."

6. Parham et al. (2006) "Prevalence and Predictors of Squamous Intraepithelial Lesions of the Cervix in HIV-Infected Women in Lusaka, Zambia."

7. Ibid.

8. Groesbeck Parham, personal communication.

9. CIDRZ, "Training."

10. Groesbeck Parham, personal communication.

11. Ibid.

12. Dr. Parham was joined by a leadership team of Zambian health providers, including Dr. Mulindi Mwanahamuntu, head of Gynecology at the University Teaching Hospital at the University of Zambia; Dr. Sharon Kampambwe, the team's lead physician-administrator; Dr. Kennedy Lishimpi, the director of the Cancer Diseases Hospital; and the nursing team.

13. Pink Ribbon Red Ribbon, "About the Partnership."

14. JHPIEGO, an NGO affiliated with Johns Hopkins, began work on VIA in Zimbabwe in 1995. It also does work in Burkina Faso and Haiti. Work was done even earlier in South Africa, India, Italy, and the U.S. (visual inspection of the uterine cervix with acetic acid). Johns Hopkins worked in Thailand. Partners in Health worked in Haiti and El Salvador, Lestho, Malawi, and Rwanda. Efforts are currently under way in Kenya, Tanzania, Uganda, Botswana, Ghana, Nigeria, India, Vietnam, and Haiti, among others.

15. Only a minority of these cases will be positive in HIV-negative women, requiring follow-up with VIA. Results from samples collected by women on themselves are nearly as good as those collected by health care providers. Currently, however, this project is not approved for self-collection: Qiao et al. (2008) "A New HPV-DNA Test for Cervical-Cancer Screening in Developing Regions: A Cross-Sectional Study of Clinical Accuracy in Rural China"; personal communication with Irma Alfaro-Beitz, Sr., Director Global Health, Qiagen Inc., December 18, 2012; and with Jose Jeronimo, Associate Director, PATH, December 16, 2012.

16. GAVI Alliance (2012) "More Than 30 Million Girls to Be Immunised with HPV Vaccines by 2020 with GAVI Support."

17. Groesbeck Parham, personal communication.

18. WHO (2011) *Global HIV/AIDS Response: Epidemic Update and Health Sector Progress Towards Universal Access: Progress Report 2011.*

19. WHO (2012) "HIV/AIDS Factsheet"; Lozano et al. (2012) "Global and Regional Mortality from 235 Causes of Death for 20 Age Groups in 1990 and 2010."

20. WHO (2012) "HIV/AIDS Factsheet"; WHO (2011) *Global HIV/AIDS Response: Epidemic Update and Health Sector Progress Towards Universal Access: Progress Report 2011.*

21. WHO (2012) "HIV/AIDS Factsheet"; WHO (2011) *Global HIV/AIDS Response Epidemic Update and Health Sector Progress towards Universal Access*; UNAIDS (2011) *HIV AIDS: How to Get to Zero: Faster. Smarter. Better.*

22. Marseille, Hofmann, and Kahn (2002) "HIV Prevention before HAART in Sub-Saharan Africa."

23. Connor, Rafter, and Rodgers (2004) "Do Fixed-Dose Combination Pills or Unit-of-Use Packaging Improve Adherence? A Systematic Review."

24. UNAIDS (2012) *Together We Will End AIDS.*

25. Topp et al. (2010) "Strengthening Health Systems at Facility-Level: Feasibility of Integrating Antiretroviral Therapy into Primary Health Care Services in Lusaka, Zambia."

26. Pfeiffer et al. (2010) "Integration of HIV/AIDS Services into African Pri-

mary Health Care: Lessons Learned for Health System Strengthening in Mozambique: A Case Study."

27. Topp et al. (2012) "Integrating HIV Treatment with Primary Care Outpatient Services: Opportunities and Challenges from a Scaled-up Model in Zambia."

28. Callaghan, Ford, and Schneider (2010) "A Systematic Review of Task-Shifting for HIV Treatment and Care in Africa."

29. Robinson (2001) "Nkosi Johnson."

30. Lester et al. (2010) "Effects of a Mobile Phone Short Message Service on Antiretroviral Treatment Adherence in Kenya (Weltel Kenya): A Randomised Trial"; Pop-Eleches et al. (2011) "Mobile Phone Technologies Improve Adherence to Antiretroviral Treatment in a Resource-Limited Setting: A Randomized Controlled Trial of Text Message Reminders"; WHO (2011) *mHealth: New Horizons for Health through Mobile Technologies*; Piette et al. (2012) *"Impacts of e-Health on the Outcomes of Care in Low- and Middle-Income Countries: Where Do We Go from Here?"*

31. United Nations Maternal Health Task Force and Global Health Visions (2012) *UN Commission on Life-Saving Commodities for Women and Children: Country Case Studies*; Qiang et al. (2012) *Mobile Applications for the Health Sector*.

32. Novartis, "SMS for Life."

33. Barrington et al. (2010) "SMS for Life: A Pilot Project to Improve Anti-Malarial Drug Supply Management in Tanzania Using Standard Technology."

34. Sudio et al. (2012) "The Magnitude and Trend of Artemether-Lumefantrine Stock-outs at Public Health Facilities in Kenya 2012."

35. Ibrahim (2009) *Health Systems, Information Flows, and Technology Choices: The Promise of eHealth in Africa*.

36. Harris, Stevens, and Morris (2009) "Keeping It Real: Combating the Spread of Fake Drugs"; WHO (2012) *Survey of the Quality of Selected Antimalarial Medicines Circulating in Six Countries of Sub-Saharan Africa*.

37. Hopkins et al. (2008) Rapid Diagnostic Tests for Malaria at Sites of Varying Transmission Intensity in Uganda"; Makuwa et al. (2002) "Reliability of Rapid Diagnostic Tests for HIV Variant Infection"; Lien et al. (2000) "Evaluation of Rapid Diagnostic Tests for the Detection of Human Immunodeficiency Virus Types 1 and 2, Hepatitis B Surface Antigen, and Syphilis in Ho Chi Minh City, Vietnam"; Dinnes et al. (2007) "A Systematic Review of Rapid Diagnostic Tests for the Detection of Tuberculosis Infection"; Clement, Dewint, and Leroux-Roels (2002) "Evaluation of a New Rapid Test for the Combined Detection of Hepatitis B Virus Surface Antigen and Hepatitis B Virus E Antigen."

38. Mavandadi et al. (2012) "A Mathematical Framework for Combining Decisions of Multiple Experts toward Accurate and Remote Diagnosis of Malaria Using Tele-Microscopy."

Notes to Chapter 7

1. Lozano et al. (2012) "Global and Regional Mortality from 235 Causes of Death for 20 Age Groups in 1990 and 2010"; WHO (2011) *Global Status Report on Noncommunicable Diseases 2010.*
2. Bloom et al. (2011) *The Global Burden of Noncommunicable Diseases.*
3. Lozano et al. (2012) "Global and Regional Mortality from 235 Causes of Death for 20 Age Groups in 1990 and 2010"; WHO (2011) "Fact Sheet: The Top 10 Causes of Death"; Mackay and Mensah (2004) *The Atlas of Heart Disease and Stroke.*
4. Haskell (2003) "Cardiovascular Disease Prevention and Lifestyle Interventions: Effectiveness and Efficacy"; Rothwell et al. (2012) "Effect of Daily Aspirin on Risk of Cancer Metastasis"; Rothwell et al. (2012) "Short-Term Effects of Daily Aspirin on Cancer Incidence, Mortality, and Non-Vascular Death"; Raju et al. (2011) "Effect of Aspirin on Mortality in the Primary Prevention of Cardiovascular Disease"; WHO (2007) *Prevention of Cardiovascular Disease: Guidelines for Assessment and Management of Cardiovascular Risk.*
5. Christakis (2007) "The Spread of Obesity in a Large Social Network over 32 Years"; Biglan et al. (1995) "Peer and Parental Influences on Adolescent Tobacco Use."
6. Lewin et al. (2010) "Lay Health Workers in Primary and Community Health Care for Maternal and Child Health and the Management of Infectious Disease."
7. Haines et al. (2007) "Achieving Child Survival Goals: Potential Contribution of Community Health Workers."
8. India Knowledge@Wharton (2010) "Narayana Hrudayalaya: A Model for Accessible, Affordable Health Care?"
9. Ibid.; Clover (2012) "'In 10 Years' Time, Doctors Will Require a Second Opinion from a Computer."
10. Kothandaraman and Mookerjee (2007) *Case Study: Healthcare for All: Narayana, Hrudayalaya, Bangalore*; Rego and Bhandary (2006) "New model: A social entrepreneur changes the landscape."
11. Salter (2012) "The World's 50 Most Innovative Companies: Narayana Hruduyalaya Hospitals"; India Knowledge@Wharton (2010) "Narayana Hrudayalaya."
12. Salter (2012) "The World's 50 Most Innovative Companies."
13. Kothandaraman and Mookerjee (2007) *Case Study: Healthcare for All;* Salter

(2012) "The World's 50 Most Innovative Companies"; Narayana Hrudayalaya Hospitals, "Telemedicine."

14. Salter (2012) "The World's 50 Most Innovative Companies."

15. Kothandaraman and Mookerjee (2007) *Case Study: Healthcare for All.*

16. Ascension Health (2012) "Narayana Hrudayalaya Hospitals Team with
Ascension Health Alliance to Build Health City at Grand Cayman."

17. Kothandaraman and Mookerjee (2007) *Case Study: Healthcare for All.*

18. Aravind Eye Care System "Clinical Services": Vickers (2011) *Driving Down
the Cost of High-Quality Care: Lessons from the Aravind Eye Care System.*

19. Vickers (2011) *Driving Down the Cost of High-Quality Care.*

20. National Eye Institute and Lions Clubs International Foundation (2008) *NEI
2005 Survey of Public Knowledge, Attitude, and Practices Related to Eye Health
and Disease.*

21. WHO (2012) *Global Data on Visual Impairments 2010.*

22. Gordois, Pezzullo, and Cutler (2010) "The Global Economic Cost of Visual
Impairment."

23. WHO (2012) "Visual Impairment and Blindness Fact Sheet."

24. VisionSpring, "VisionSpring at a Glance."

25. VisionSpring, "The Vision Entrepreneur."

26. VisionSpring, "Partners: BRAC."

27. The Global Health Group (2012) *Clinical Social Franchising Compendium.*

28. Glenton et al. (2010) "The Female Community Health Volunteer Programme in Nepal: Decision Makers' Perceptions of Volunteerism, Payment and Other Incentives"; USAID (2009) *A Vision for Health: Performance-
Based Financing in Rwanda.*

29. WHO (2012) "Depression Fact Sheet."

30. Murray et al. (2012) "Disability-Adjusted Life Years (DALYs) for 291 Diseases and Injuries in 21 Regions, 1990–2010: A Systematic Analysis for the
Global Burden of Disease Study 2010."

31. Lozano et al. (2012) "Global and Regional Mortality from 235 Causes of
Death for 20 Age Groups in 1990 and 2010."

32. Ibid.

33. Patel et al. (2010) "Effectiveness of an Intervention Led by Lay Health
Counsellors for Depressive and Anxiety Disorders in Primary Care in Goa,
India (MANAS): A Cluster-Randomised Controlled Trial."

34. Rahman et al. (2008) "Cognitive Behaviour Therapy-Based Intervention by
Community Health Workers for Mothers with Depression and Their Infants in Rural Pakistan: A Cluster-Randomised Controlled Trial."

35. Eaton et al. (2011) "Scale Up of Services for Mental Health in Low-Income
and Middle-Income Countries"; Manandhar et al. (2004) "Effect of a Partici-

patory Intervention with Women's Groups on Birth Outcomes in Nepal: A Cluster-Randomised Controlled Trial."

36. Bing et al. (2007) "HIV/AIDS Behavioral Surveillance among Angolan Military Men"; Bing et al. (2008) "Evaluation of a Prevention Intervention to Reduce HIV Risk among Angolan Soldiers."

37. Personal communication, Ahmed Abajobir, Country Director, Drew Cares International, Rwanda, January 14 , 2013.

Notes to Chapter 8

1. *Economist* (2012) "The Path through the Fields."
2. Deutsche Bank (2007) *Microfinance: An Emerging Investment Opportunity.*
3. W.K. Kellogg Foundation (2004) W.K. Kellogg Foundation Logic Model Development Guide.

Notes to Chapter 9

1. *Economist* (2011) "Africa's Impressive Growth."
2. Personal communication with Gina L. Tesla, Director of Corporate Citizenship Initiatives, IBM, December 20, 2012.
3. Personal communication with Heather Anderson, Vice President of Programs, Global Health Corps, December 19, 2012.

Bibliography

Abernathy, W., and J. M. Utterback. "Patterns of Industrial Innovation." *Technology Review* 80, no. 7 (1978): 40–47.

Afuah, A. *Innovation Management*. Oxford: Oxford University Press, 1998.

Ahmed, S., and M.M. Khan. "Is Demand-Side Financing Equity Enhancing? Lessons from a Maternal Health Voucher Scheme in Bangladesh." *Soc Sci Med* 72, no. 10 (2011): 1704–10.

Aid Village Clinics. "African Infectious Disease Village Clinics." Aid Village Clinics, www.aidvillageclinics.org/.

Anderson, P., and M.L. Tushman. "Technological Discontinuities and Dominant Designs: A Cyclical Model of Technological Change." *Administrative Science Quarterly* 35, no. 4 (1990): 604–33.

Aravind Eye Care System. "Clinical Services."Aravind Eye Care Center, www.aravind.org/ClinicalServices.aspx.

Ascension Health. "Narayana Hrudayalaya Hospitals Team with Ascension Health Alliance to Build Health City at Grand Cayman." Ascension Health, April 10, 2012.

Atun, R., F.M. Knaul, Y. Akachi, and J. Frenk. "Innovative Financing for Health: What Is Truly Innovative?" *Lancet* 380 no. 9858 (2012): 2044–49.

Babycenter. "Babycenter's Maternal Health Mission." Babycenter, www.babycenter.com/mobilehealth.

Baldwin, C.Y., and K.B. Clark. *Design Rules: The Power of Modularity*. Cambridge, MA: MIT Press, 2000.

Banbury, C.M., and W. Mitchell, "The Effect of Introducing Important Incremental Innovations on Market Share and Business Survival." *Strategic Management Journal* 16 (1995): 161–82.

Banerjee, A., and E. Duflo. *Poor Economics: A Radical Rethinking of the Way to Fight Global Poverty*. New York: PublicAffairs, 2011.

Barrington, J., et al. "SMS for Life: A Pilot Project to Improve Anti-Malarial Drug Supply Management in Rural Tanzania Using Standard Technology." *Malaria Journal* 9 (2010): 298.

Baseman, J.G., and L.A. Koutsky. "The Epidemiology of Human Papillomavirus Infections." *Journal of Clinical Virology* 32 (2005): 16–24.

Bate, R. "Fake Drugs Kill the Poor." *Economic Affairs* 27 (2007): 84.

Bellows, N.M., B.W. Bellows, and C. Warren. "Systematic Review: The Use of Vouchers for Reproductive Health Services in Developing Countries: Systematic Review." *Trop Med Int Health* 16, no. 1 (2011): 84–96.

Berk, J. and A. Adhvaryu. "The Impact of a Novel Franchise Clinic Network on Access to Medicines and Vaccinations in Kenya: A Cross-Sectional Study." *BMJ Open* 2, no. 4 (2012).

Bernstein, A. *The Case for Business in Developing Economies*. New York: Penguin Books, 2010.

Bertrand, J.T., et al. "Voluntary Medical Male Circumcision: A Qualitative Study Exploring the Challenges of Costing Demand Creation in Eastern and Southern Africa." *PLOS ONE* 6, no. 11 (2011): e27562.

Beverage Industry. "Sports Drink Sales Get into Shape." *Beverage Industry*, July 12, 2011.

Bhattacharyya, O., S. Khor, A. McGahan, D. Dunne, A. S. Daar, and P. A. Singer. "Innovative Health Service Delivery Models in Low and Middle Income Countries: What Can We Learn from the Private Sector?" *Health Res Policy Syst* 8 (2010): 24.

Bicycling Empowerment Network. "Strengthening the Grassroots Response to HIV/AIDS." Windhoek, Namibia: Bicycling Empowerment Network (BEN), 2012.

Biglan, A., T.E. Duncan, D.V. Ary, and K. Smolkowski. "Peer and Parental Influences on Adolescent Tobacco Use." *Journal of Behavioral Medicine* 18, no. 4 (1995): 315–30.

Bilal, N.K., et al. "Health Extension Workers in Ethiopia: Improved Access and Coverage for the Rural Poor." *Yes, Africa Can: Success Stories from a Dynamic Continent* (2011): 433.

Binagwaho, A. "Community Health Workers in Rwanda Improve Access to Care." In *Health and Human Rights Open Forum*, 2009, www.hhropenforum.org/2009/08/chws-in-rwanda/.

Birdsall, N., and W.D. Savedoff, with A. Mahgoub and K. Vyborny. *Cash on delivery: A New Approach to Foreign Aid*. Washington, DC: Center for Global Development, 2010.

Bing, E.G., et al. "Evaluation of a Prevention Intervention to Reduce HIV Risk among Angolan Soldiers." *AIDS and Behavior* 12, no. 3 (2008): 384–95.

———. "HIV/AIDS Behavioral Surveillance among Angolan Military Men." *AIDS and Behavior* 12, no. 4 (2008): 578–84.

Bloom, D.E., et al. *The Global Economic Burden of Noncommunicable Diseases.* Geneva: World Economic Forum, 2011.

Bloom, P., and G. Dees. "Cultivate Your Ecosystem." *Stanford Social Innovation Review* 6, no. 1 (2008): 46–53.

Bloom, P., and A. Chatterji. "Scaling Social Entrepreneurial Impact." *California Management Review* 51, no. 3 (2009): 114–33.

Bodilly, S.J., and C.H. Augustine. *Revitalizing Arts Education through Community-Wide Coordination.* Arlington, VA: RAND Corporation, 2008.

BRAC. "Stay Informed: BRAC at a Glance." BRAC Communications, www.brac.net/content/stay-informed-brac-glance#.UJWuIW_A96J.

Bradach, J. "Going to Scale: The Challenge of Replicating Social Programs." *Stanford Social Innovation Review* 1, no. 1 (2003): 19–25.

Brown, J., et al. "A Hand-Powered, Portable, Low-Cost Centrifuge for Diagnosing Anemia in Low Resource Settings." *The American Journal of Tropical Medicine and Hygiene* 85, no. 2 (2011): 327–32.

Burgelman, R.A., and Y.L. Doz. "The Power of Strategic Integration." *Sloan Management Review* 42, no. 3 (2001): 28–38.

Byrne, A., and A. Morgan. "How the Integration of Traditional Birth Attendants with Formal Health Systems Can Increase Skilled Birth Attendance." *Int J Gynaecol Obstet* 115 , no. 1 (2011): 127–34.

Byrne, J.A. "The Man Who Invented Management: Why Peter Drucker's Ideas Still Matter." *Business Week* 28 (2005): 96.

Callaghan, M., N. Ford, and H. Schneider. "A Systematic Review of Task-Shifting for HIV Treatment and Care in Africa." *Human Resources for Health* 8, no. 8 (2010).

CARE International. *Annual Report 2011.* Geneva: CARE International, 2011.

Carrin, G., I. Mathauer, K. Xu, and D.B. Evans. "Universal Coverage of Health Services: Tailoring Its Implementation." *Bulletin of the World Health Organization* 86, no. 11 (November 2008): 817–908.

Center for Infectious Disease Research in Zambia. "Training: CIDRZ." Centre for Infectious Disease Research in Zambia, www.cidrz.org.

Central Statistical Agency of Ethiopia. *Ethiopia Demographic and Health Survey 2011.* Addis Ababa, Ethiopia: Central Statistical Agency of Ethiopia, 2012.

Chen, S., and M. Ravallion. "The Developing World Is Poorer Than We Thought, But No Less Successful in the Fight Against Poverty." *Quarterly Journal of Economics* 125, no. 4 (2010): 1577–1625.

Chib, A. *Information and Communication Technologies for Health Care: Midwife Mobile-Phone Project in Aceh Besar.* Federal Way, WA: World Vision, 2008.

Chibanda, D., et al. "Problem-Solving Therapy for Depression and Common Mental Disorders in Zimbabwe: Piloting a Task-Shifting Primary Mental Health Care Intervention in a Population with a High Prevalence of People Living with HIV." BMC Public Health 11:828 (2011), www.biomedcentral. com/1471-2458/11/828.

Chimombo, J.P.G. "Quantity Versus Quality in Education: Case Studies in Malawi." *International Review of Education* 51, no. 2/3 (2005): 155–72.

Choi, H.W., et al. "The Effectiveness of Insecticide-Impregnated Bed Nets in Reducing Cases of Malaria Infection: A Meta-Analysis of Published Results." *American Journal of Tropical Medicine and Hygiene* 52, no. 2 (1995): 377–82.

Christakis, N.A., and J. H. Fowler. "The Spread of Obesity in a Large Social Network over 32 Years." *New England Journal of Medicine* 357, no. 4 (2007): 370–79.

Christensen, C., and R. Rosenbloom. "Explaining the Attacker's Advantage: Technological Paradigms, Organizational Dynamics and the Value Network." *Research Policy* 24 (1995): 233–57.

Chuma, J., V. Okungu, J. Ntwiga, and C. Molyneux. "Towards Achieving Abuja Targets: Identifying and Addressing Barriers to Access and Use of Insecticides Treated Nets among the Poorest Populations in Kenya." *BMC Public Health* 10, no. 1 (2010): 137.

Clark, C.H., C. Massarsky, T.S. Raben, and E. Warsham. *Scaling Social Impact: A Literature Toolkit for Funders.* Durham, NC: Duke University and Growth Philanthropy Network, 2012.

Clement, F., P. Dewint, and G. Leroux-Roels. "Evaluation of a New Rapid Test for the Combined Detection of Hepatitis B Virus Surface Antigen and Hepatitis B Virus E Antigen." *Journal of Clinical Microbiology* 40, no. 12 (2002): 4603–606.

Clover, B. "In 10 Years' Time, Doctors Will Require a Second Opinion from a Computer." *Health Service Journal,* April 26, 2012, www.hsj.co.uk/leadership/ outside-the-box/in-10-years-time-doctors-will-require-a-second-opinion-from-a-computer/5043864.article.

Coca-Cola Company. "Coca-Cola Announces Long-Term Partnership with DEKA R&D to Help Bring Clean Water to Communities in Need." Atlanta, GA: Coca-Cola Company, September 25, 2012.

Colclough, C. *Marketizing Education and Health in Developing Countries: Miracle or Mirage?* New York: Oxford University Press, 1998.

Cole, R.E. "Learning from the Quality Movement: What Did and Didn't Happen and Why?" *California Management Review* 41, no. 1 (1998): 43–74.

Coleman, A. *Riders for Health: Health Care Distribution Solutions in Sub-Saharan Africa.* Case #GS-58. Stanford, CA: Stanford Graduate School of Business, 2007.

Collier, P. *The Bottom Billion: Why the Poorest Countries Are Failing and What Can Be Done about It.* New York: Oxford University Press, 2007.

Connor, J., N. Rafter, and A. Rodgers. "Do Fixed-Dose Combination Pills or Unit-of-Use Packaging Improve Adherence? A Systematic Review." *Bulletin of the World Health Organization* 82, no. 12 (2004): 935–39.

Consultative Group to Assist the Poor. *Advancing Financial Access for the World's Poor.* Washington, D.C.: CGAP, 2011.

Cooper, R., R.E. Slavin, and N.A. Madden. "Success for All: Improving the Quality of Implementation of Whole-School Change through the Use of a National Reform Network." *Education and Urban Society* 30, no. 3 (1998): 385–408.

Cooper, A., and C. Smith. "How Established Firms Respond to Threatening Technologies," *Academy of Management Executive* 6, no. 2 (1992): 55–70

Creanga, A., Gillespie, Karklins, and Tsui. "Low Use of Contraception among Poor Women in Africa: An Equity Issue." *Bulletin of the World Health Organization* 89, no. 4 (2011): 258 66.

Crutchfield, L., and H.M. Grant. *Forces for Good: The Six Practices of High-Impact Nonprofits.* San Francisco, CA: Jossey-Bass, 2007.

Curci, M. "Task Shifting Overcomes the Limitations of Volunteerism in Developing Nations." *Bulletin of the American College of Surgeons* (2012).

Curtis, C., et al. "Scaling-Up Coverage with Insecticide-Treated Nets against Malaria in Africa: Who Should Pay?" *The Lancet Infectious Diseases* 3, no. 5 (2003): 304–7.

Damanpour, F. "Organizational Complexity and Innovation: Developing and Testing Contingency Models." *Management Science* 42, no. 5 (1996): 693–701.

Dandona, R., et al. "Refractive Error in Children in a Rural Population in India." *Investigative Ophthalmology & Visual Science* 43, no. 3 (2002): 615–22.

Datnow, A., L. Hubbard, and H. Mehan. *Extending Educational Reform: From One School to Many.* New York: Psychology Press, 2002.

Davila, T., M.J. Epstein, and R. Shelton. *Making Innovation Work: How to Manage It, Measure It, and Profit from It.* Upper Saddle River, NJ: Pearson, 2013.

Day, G.S., and P.J.H. Schoemaker. "Avoiding the Pitfalls of Emerging Technologies," *California Management Review* 42, no. 2 (2000): 8–33.

De Mel, S., D. McKenzie, and C. Woodruff. "Returns to Capital in Microenterprises: Evidence from a Field Experiment." *Quarterly Journal of Economics* 123, no. 4 (2008): 1329–72.

Dewar, R.D., and J.E. Dutton. "The Adoption of Radical and Incremental Innovations: An Empirical Analysis." *Management Science* 32, no. 11 (1986): 1422–33.

Dieckmann, R. "Microfinance: An Emerging Investment Opportunity." *Deutsche Bank Research*, 2007.

Dinnes, J., et al. "A Systematic Review of Rapid Diagnostic Tests for the Detection of Tuberculosis Infection." *Health Technology Assessment* 11, no. 3 (2007): 1–196.

Docherty, J.P., R.C. Surles, and C.M. Donovan. "Organizational Theory." Chapter 3 in *Textbook of Administrative Psychiatry*, ed. by J. Talbott and R. Hales, 33–41. Arlington, VA: American Psychiatric Publishing, 2001.

Dougherty, D., and C. Hardy. "Sustained Product Innovation in Large, Mature Organizations: Overcoming Innovation-to-Organization Problems," *Academy of Management Journal* 39 (1996): 1120–53.

Drucker, P.F. "The Discipline of Innovation." *Harvard Business Review* 63, no. 3 (August 2002): 67–72.

Dunham, W. "Bush Signs Expansion of Global AIDS Programs." *Reuters*, July 30, 2008.

Dybul, M. "Finding Common Ground to Save the Lives of Women and Child and Create Happy, Healthy Families." *Huffington Post*, July 9, 2012.

Dybul, M., P. Piot, and J. Frenk. "Reshaping Global Health." *Policy Review* 173, no. 1 (2012).

E Health Point. "About Us." E Health Point. http://ehealthpoint.com/?page_id=5.

———. "E HealthPoint." E Health Point, August 2012. http://ehealthpoint.com/wp-content/uploads/2012/09/E-HEALTHPOINT-Aug-2012.pdf.

Earth Institute. *One Million Community Health Workers: Technical Task Force Report*. New York: Earth Institute, 2011.

Easterly, W. *The White Man's Burden: Why the West's Efforts to Aid the Rest Have Done So Much Ill and So Little Good*. New York: Penguin Press, 2006.

Eaton, J., et al. "Scale Up of Services for Mental Health in Low-Income and Middle-Income Countries." *Lancet* 378, no. 9802 (2011): 1592–1603.

Economist. "Africa's Impressive Growth." *Economist*, January 6, 2011.

———. "First Break All the Rules: The Charms of Frugal Innovation." *Economist*, April 15, 2010.

———. "The Path Through the Fields." *Economist*, November 3, 2012.

Ehrbeck, T., N. Henke, and T. Kibasi. "The Emerging Market in Health Care Innovation." *McKinsey Quarterly* (2010).

Ehrenberg, E. "On the Definition and Measurement of Technological Discontinuities." *Technovation* 15 (1995): 437–52.

Ekirapa-Kiracho, E., et al. "Increasing Access to Institutional Deliveries Using Demand and Supply Side Incentives: Early Results from a Quasi-Experimental Study: An Innovative Approach to Building Capacity at an African University to Improve Health Outcomes." *BMC International Health and Human Rights 2011*, no. 1 (2011).

Elmore, R. "Getting to Scale with Good Educational Practice." *Harvard Educational Review* 66, no. 1 (1996): 1–27.

Epstein, H. *The Invisible Cure: Africa, the West, and the Fight against AIDS.* New York: Farrar, Straus and Giroux, 2007.

Epstein, M.J. *Making Sustainability Work: Best Practices in Managing and Measuring Corporate Social, Environmental and Economic Impacts.* San Francisco: Berrett-Koehler, 2008.

Epstein, M.J., and E.G. Bing. "Delivering Health Care to the Global Poor: Solving the Accessibility Problem." *Innovations* 6, no. 2 (2011): 117–41.

Epstein, M.J., and B. Birchard. *Counting What Counts: Turning Corporate Accountability to Competitive Advantage.* Reading, MA: Perseus, 1999.

Epstein, M.J., and F.W. McFarlan. *Joining a Nonprofit Board: What You Need to Know.* San Francisco: Jossey-Bass, 2011.

Epstein, M.J., and K. Yuthas. "Scaling Effective Education for the Poor in Developing Countries: A Report from the Field." *Journal of Public Policy & Marketing* 31, no. 1 (2012): 102–14.

Ettlie, J.E., W.P. Bridges, and R.D. O'Keefe, "Organizational Strategy and Structural Differences for Radical versus Incremental Innovation." *Management Science* 30 (1984): 682–95.

Fairall, L., et al. "Task Shifting of Antiretroviral Treatment from Doctors to Primary-Care Nurses in South Africa (STRETCH): A Pragmatic, Parallel, Cluster-Randomised Trial." *Lancet* 380, no. 9845 (2012): 889–98.

Fairbourne, J.S., S.W. Gibson, and W.G. Dyer. *MicroFranchising: Creating Wealth at the Bottom of the Pyramid.* Cheltenham, UK: Edward Elgar, 2007.

Farmer, P. et al. "Expansion of Cancer Care and Control in Countries of Low and Middle Income: A Call to Action." *Lancet* 376, no. 9747 (2010): 1186–93.

Feachem, R.G.A., and The Malaria Elimination Group. *Shrinking the Malaria Map: A Guide on Malaria Elimination for Policy Makers.* San Francisco: Global Health Group, UCSF Global Health Sciences, 2009.

Fertig, M., and H. Tzaras. "Franchising Health Care for Kenya: The HealthStore Foundation Model." In *Microfranchising: Creating Wealth at the Bottom of the Pyramid*, ed. by J.S. Fairbourne, S.W. Gibson, and W.G. Dyer, 164–82. Northampton, MA: Edward Elgar, 2007.

———. *What Works: HealthStore's Franchise Approach to Healthcare.* Washington, DC: USAID and World Resources Institute, 2005.

Foster, R.N. *Innovation: The Attacker's Advantage.* New York: Summit, 1986.

Frenk, J. "Globalization, Health, and the Role of Telemedicine." *Telemedicine Journal & e-Health* 11, no. 3 (2005): 291–95.

————. "Reinventing Primary Health Care: The Need for Systems Integration." *Lancet* 374, no. 9684 (2009): 170–73.

Fried, L.P., P. Piot, H.C. Spencer, and R. Parker. "The Changing Landscape of Global Public Health." *Global Public Health* 7, no. 1 (2012): 1–4.

Frost, L.J., and M.R. Reich. *Access: How Do Good Health Technologies Get to Poor People in Poor Countries?* Harvard Center for Population and Development Studies, 2008.

Fudong, F. "A Relay Race to Save Lives During Bandhs." USAID, http://blog.usaid.gov/2012/08/a-relay-race-to-save-lives-during-bandhs/.

Fullan, M. *The New Meaning of Education Change*, 4th ed. New York: Teachers College Press, 2007.

————. "The Return of Large-Scale Reform." *Journal of Educational Change* 1, no. 1 (2000): 5–27.

————. "The Role of Leadership in the Promotion of Knowledge Management in Schools." *Teachers and Teaching* 8, no. 3 (2002): 409–19.

GAVI Alliance. "GAVI Alliance Progress Report 2010." Geneva: GAVI, 2010.

————. "GAVI's Impact: Saving Lives." GAVI, www.gavialliance.org/about/mission/impact/.

————. "More Than 30 Million Girls to Be Immunised with HPV Vaccines by 2020 with GAVI Support." Geneva: GAVI, December 6, 2012.

————. *Progress Report 2011*. Geneva: GAVI, 2011.

General Electric. *Healthymagination 2010 Annual Report*. Fairfield, CT: General Electric Company, 2010.

Geoghegan, T. "Frontline Health Workers: The Best Way to Save Lives, Accelerate Progress on Global Health, and Help Advance U.S. Interests." Frontline Health Workers Coalition, 2012.

Gertler, P., and C. Vermeersch. "Using Performance Incentives to Improve Health Outcomes." Washington, DC: World Bank, 2012.

Glennan, T.K., S.J. Bodilly, J.R. Galegher, and K.A. Kerr. *Expanding the Reach of Education Reforms: Perspectives from Leaders in the Scale-up of Educational Interventions*. Arlington, VA: RAND Corporation, 2004.

Glenton, C., et al. "The Female Community Health Volunteer Programme in Nepal: Decision Makers' Perceptions of Volunteerism, Payment and Other Incentives." *Soc Sci Med* 70, no. 12 (2010): 1920–27.

Global Fund to Fight AIDS, Tuberculosis and Malaria. *Monitoring and Evaluation Toolkit: HIV, Tuberculosis, Malaria, and Health and Community Systems Strengthening*. Geneva: Global Fund to Fight AIDS, Tuberculosis and Malaria, 2011.

Global Health Group. *Clinical Social Franchising Compendium: An Annual Survey of Programs, 2012*. San Francisco: Global Health Group, 2012.

————. *Clinical Social Franchising Case Study Series: Smiling Sun Franchise Program Bangladesh*. San Francisco: Global Health Group, 2011.

Globocan. "Cervical Cancer Incidence, Mortality and Prevalence Worldwide in 2008." Globocan, http://globocan.iarc.fr.

Gordois, A., L. Pezzullo, and H. Cutler. "The Global Economic Cost of Visual Impairment." Sydney, Australia: Access Economics, 2010.

Govindarajan, V., and C. Trimble. *Reverse Innovation: Create Far from Home, Win Everywhere.* Boston: Harvard Business Review Press, 2012.

Green, S., M. Gavin, and L. Aiman-Smith. "Assessing a Multidimensional Measure of Radical Innovation." *IEEE Transactions Engineering Management* 42, no. 3 (1995): 203–14.

Guttmacher Institute. "Family Planning Can Reduce High Infant Mortality Levels." Guttmacher Institute, April 2002. www.guttmacher.org/pubs/ib_2-02.html.

Haines, A., et al. "Achieving Child Survival Goals: Potential Contribution of Community Health Workers." *Lancet* 369, no. 9579 (2007): 2121–31.

Hamel, G., and C.K. Prahalad, *Competing for the Future* (Boston: Harvard Business School Press, 1994).

Hammond, A.L., et al. *The Next 4 Billion: Market Size and Business Strategy at the Base of the Pyramid.* Washington, DC: World Resources Institute and International Finance Corporation, 2007.

Haskell, W.L. "Cardiovascular Disease Prevention and Lifestyle Interventions: Effectiveness and Efficacy." *Journal of Cardiovascular Nursing* 18, no. 4 (September/October 2003): 245–55.

Haynes, A.B., et al. "A Surgical Safety Checklist to Reduce Morbidity and Mortality in a Global Population." *New England Journal of Medicine* 360 (2009): 491–99.

Health Logistics Quarterly. "USAID Deliver Project Provides Technical Assistance to the Pharmaceutical Fund and Supply Agency (PFSA)." *Health Logistics Quarterly* 2, no. 1 (2010): 1–6.

Health Unbound. "MAMA: Mobile Alliance for Maternal Action." Health Unbound, http://healthunbound.org/mama/.

Henderson, R.M., and K.B. Clark. "Architectural Innovation: The Reconfiguration of Existing Product Technologies and the Failure of Established Firms." *Administrative Science Quarterly* 35, no. 1 (1990): 9–30.

Hoffman, J. "Lifestraw Saves Those without Access to Clean Drinking Water." *New York Times*, September 26, 2009.

Holmes, D. "Rwanda: An Injection of Hope." *Lancet* 376, no. 9745 (2010): 945–46.

Hongoro, C., and L. Kumaranayake. "Do They Work? Regulating For-Profit Providers in Zimbabwe." *Health Policy and Planning* 15 (2000): 368–77.

Hopkins, H., et al. "Rapid Diagnostic Tests for Malaria at Sites of Varying Transmission Intensity in Uganda." *Journal of Infectious Diseases* 197, no. 4 (2008): 510–18.

Horton, R., et al. "GBD 2010: Understanding Disease, Injury, and Risk." *Lancet* 380, no. 9859 (2012): 2053–54.

Howitt, P., et al. "Technologies for Global Health." *Lancet* 380, no. 9840 (2012): 507–35.

Ibrajim, M. "Health Systems, Information Flows, and Technology Choices: The Promise of eHealth in Africa." Washington, DC: World Bank, 2009.

Immelt, J.R., V. Govindarajan, and C. Trimble. "How GE Is Disrupting Itself." *Harvard Business Review* (October 2009).

IndiaKnowledge@Wharton. "Narayana Hrudayalaya: A Model for Accessible, Affordable Health Care?" *IndiaKnowledge@Wharton*, July 1, 2010. http://knowledge.wharton.upenn.edu/india/article.cfm?articleid=4493.

Institute for Health Metrics and Evaluation. *Financing Global Health 2011: Continued Growth as MDG Deadline Approaches*. Seattle: IHME, 2011.

Institute of Medicine Roundtable on Evidence-Based Medicine. "Missed Prevention Opportunities." In *The Healthcare Imperative: Lowering Costs and Improving Outcomes Workshop Series Summary*. Washington, DC: National Academy of Science, 2010.

International Association of Physicians in AIDS Care. *Multidisciplinary Care Teams: Report of an IAPAC Consultation in Addis Ababa, Ethiopia*. Chicago: International Association of Physicians in AIDS Care, 2011.

International Federation of Red Cross and Red Crescent Societies. *Malaria Prevention in the Community: Training Guide for Red Cross Red Crescent Supervisors and Volunteers*. Geneva: International Federation of Red Cross and Red Crescent Societies, 2009.

International Finance Corporation, *The Business of Health in Africa: Partnering with the Private Sector to Improve People's Lives*. Washington, DC: IFC, 2007, www.ifc.org/ifcext/healthinafrica.nsf/Content/FullReport.

Iqbal A., S. Rasheed, S.M.A. Hanifi, and A. Bhuiya. "Reaching the Poor with Performance Based Payment for Safe Delivery Services in Rural Bangladesh." *Bulletin of Medicus Mundi Switzerland*, no. 112 (April 2009).

Joint Learning Network for Universal Health Coverage. "Rwanda: Mutuelles de Santé." Joint Learning Network for Universal Health Coverage, www.jointlearningnetwork.org/content/mutuelles-de-sante.

Jokhio, A.H., H.R. Winter, and K.K. Cheng. "An Intervention Involving Traditional Birth Attendants and Perinatal and Maternal Mortality in Pakistan." *New England Journal of Medicine*, no. 352 (2005).

Juran, J.M. *Juran on Quality by Design: The New Steps for Planning Quality into Goods and Services*. New York: The Free Press, 1992.

Kanani, R. "Jaipur Foot: One of the Most Technologically Advanced Social Enterprises in the World." *Forbes*, August 8, 2011.

Kantamara, P., P. Hallinger, and M. Jatiket. "Scaling-up Education Reform in Thailand: Context, Collaboration, Networks and Change." *Planning and Changing* 37, no. 1 (2006): 5–23.

Karlan, D., D.S. Karlan, and J. Appel. *More Than Good Intentions: How a New Economics Is Helping to Solve Global Poverty*. New York: Dutton, 2011.

Katayama, L. "How Health Care Nonprofit Living Goods Learned a Lesson from Avon Ladies." Fast Company, www.fastcompany.com/1709280/how-health-care-nonprofit-living-goods-learned-lesson-avon-ladies.

Kenya Ministry of Health and National AIDS and STI Control Programme. *Kenya AIDS Indicator Survey 2007 Final Report*. Nairobi, Kenya: NASCOP, 2007.

Kenya National Bureau of Statistics and ICF Macro. *2008–09 Kenya Demographic and Health Survey: Key Findings*. Calverton, MD: KNBS and ICF Macro, 2010.

Khanna, T., and T. Bijlani. "Narayana Hrudayalaya Heart Hospital: Cardiac Care for the Poor (B)." *Harvard Business School Supplement* (2011), Case No. 712-402.

Khatib, R.A., et al. "Markets, Voucher Subsidies and Free Nets Combine to Achieve High Bed Net Coverage in Rural Tanzania." *Malar J* 7 (2008): 98.

Kirby, S.N., M. Berends, and S. Naftel. *Implementation in a Longitudinal Sample of New American Schools: Four Years into Scale-Up*. Arlington, VA: RAND, 2001.

Kirk, G.V. "The MicroConsignment Model: Bridging the 'Last Mile' of Access to Products and Services for the Rural Poor," *Innovations* 5 (2010): 101–27.

Kitchener, H.C., P.E. Castle, and J.T. Cox. "Achievements and Limitations of Cervical Cytology Screening." *Vaccine* 24 (2006): S63–S70.

Knaul, F.M., et al. "Meeting the Emerging Challenge of Breast and Cervical Cancer in Low- and Middle-Income Countries." *International Journal of Gynecology & Obstetrics* (2012).

Kothandaraman, P., and S. Mookerjee. "Case Study: Healthcare for All: Narayana, Hrudayalaya, Bangalore." In *Growing Inclusive Markets: Business Works for Development, Development Works for Business*. New York: United Nations Development Programme, 2007.

Kreiss, J.K., et al. "Human Immunodeficiency Virus, Human Papillomavirus, and Cervical Intraepithelian Neoplasia in Nairobi Prostitutes." *Sexually Transmitted Diseases* 19, no 1 (1992): 54–59.

Kristof, N.D., and S. WuDunn. *Half the Sky: Turning Oppression into Opportunity for Women Worldwide*. New York: Alfred A. Knopf, 2009.

LaFrance, S., et al. *Scaling Capacities: Supports for Growing Impact*. Working paper, LaFrance, 2006.

Leach-Kemon, K., et al. "The Global Financial Crisis Has Led to a Slowdown in Growth of Funding to Improve Health in Many Developing Countries." *Health Affairs* 31, no. 1 (2012): 228–35.

Lehr, David. "Microfranchising at the Base of the Pyramid." New York: Acumen Fund (2008).

Lester, R.T., et al. "Effects of a Mobile Phone Short Message Service on Antiretroviral Treatment Adherence in Kenya (Weltel Kenya): A Randomised Trial." *Lancet* 376, no. 9755 (2010): 1838–45.

Lewin, S., et al. "Lay Health Workers in Primary and Community Health Care for Maternal and Child Health and the Management of Infectious Disease." *Cochrane Database of Systematic Reviews* 3 (2010).

Lien, T.X., et al. "Evaluation of Rapid Diagnostic Tests for the Detection of Human Immunodeficiency Virus Types 1 And 2, Hepatitis B Surface Antigen, and Syphilis in Ho Chi Minh City, Vietnam." *American Journal of Tropical Medicine and Hygiene* 62, no. 2 (2000): 301–9.

Loevinsohn, B., and A. Harding. "Buying Results? Contracting for Health Service Delivery in Developing Countries." *Lancet* 366, no. 9486 (2005): 676–81.

London, T. "Making Better Investments at the Bottom of the Pyramid." *Harvard Business Review* (May 2009): 106–12.

Lozano et al. "Global and Regional Mortality from 235 Causes of Death for 20 Age Groups in 1990 and 2010: A Systematic Analysis for the Global Burden of Disease Study 2010." *Lancet* 380, no. 9859 (2012): 2095–2128.

Macke, S., R. Misra, and A. Sharma. "Jaipur Foot: Challenging Convention." University of Michigan Business School (2003).

Makina, M. "Debate Rages over Traditional Birth Assistants U-Turn in Malawi." *Think Africa Press*, January 6, 2011.

Makokha, S. "Kenya: State Bans Traditional Birth Attendants in Matungu." *The Star*, July 14, 2011.

Makuwa, M., et al. "Reliability of Rapid Diagnostic Tests for HIV Variant Infection." *Journal of Virological Methods* 103, no. 2 (2002): 183–90.

Manandhar, D.S., et al. "Effect of a Participatory Intervention with Women's Groups on Birth Outcomes in Nepal: Cluster-Randomised Controlled Trial." *Lancet* 364, no. 9438 (2004): 970–79.

Mangham, L.J., and K. Hanson. "Scaling Up in International Health: What Are the Key Issues?" *Health Policy and Planning* 25, no. 2 (2010): 85–96.

Marseille, E., P.B. Hofmann, and J.G. Kahn. "HIV Prevention before HAART in Sub-Saharan Africa." *Lancet* 359, no. 9320 (2002): 1851–56.

Masum, H., et al. "Accelerating Health Product Innovation in Sub-Saharan Africa." *Innovations* 2 (2007): 129–49.

Mavandadi, S., et al. "A Mathematical Framework for Combining Decisions of Multiple Experts toward Accurate and Remote Diagnosis of Malaria Using Tele-Microscopy." *PLOS ONE* 7, no. 10 (2012): e46192.

Mayne, S.T., et al. "Nutrient Intake and Risk of Subtypes of Esophageal and

Gastric Cancer." *Cancer Epidemiology, Biomarkers & Prevention* 10, no. 10 (2001): 1055–62.

McKay, J., and G. Mensah. *The Atlas of Heart Disease and Stroke*. Geneva: WHO, 2004.

Mechael, P.N. "The Case for mHealth in Developing Countries." *Innovations* 4 (2009): 103–18.

Mehta, P.K., and S. Shenoy. *Infinite Vision*. San Francisco: Berrett-Koehler, 2011.

Meuwissen, L.E., A.C. Gorter, A.D.M. Kester, and J.A. Knottnerus. "Does a Competitive Voucher Program for Adolescents Improve the Quality of Reproductive Health Care? A Simulated Patient Study in Nicaragua." *BMC Public Health* 6 (2006): 204.

Moyo, D. *Dead Aid: Why Aid Is Not Working and How There Is a Better Way for Africa*. New York: Farrar, Straus and Giroux, 2009.

Mugeni, C., F. Ngabo, and J. Humuza. "Community Performance-Based Financing in Health: Incentivizing Mothers and Community Health Workers to Improve Maternal Health Outcomes in Rwanda." In *Final Report: World Conference on Social Determinants of Health*, Rio De Janeiro, Brazil, 2011 (Geneva: WHO, 2012).

Munos, M.K., C.L. Walker, and R.E. Black. "The Effect of Oral Rehydration Solution and Recommended Home Fluids on Diarrhoea Mortality." *Oxford Journals: International Journal of Epidemiology* 39, no. suppl. 1 (2010): 175–87.

Murray, C.J., and J. Frenk. "Health Metrics and Evaluation: Strengthening the Science." *Lancet* 371, no. 9619 (2008): 1191–99.

Murray, C.J., et al. "Disability-Adjusted Life Years (DALYs) for 291 Diseases and Injuries in 21 Regions, 1990–2010: A Systematic Analysis for the Global Burden of Disease Study 2010." *Lancet* 380, no. 9859 (2012): 2197–223.

Mwandi, Z., et al. "Voluntary Medical Male Circumcision: Translating Research into the Rapid Expansion of Services in Kenya, 2008–2011." *PLoS medicine* 8, no. 11 (2011): e1001130.

Narayana Hrudayalaya Hospitals. "Telemedicine." Narayana Hrudayalaya Hospitals, www.narayanahospitals.com/services/telemedicine/#.

National Eye Institute. "2005 Survey of Public Knowledge, Attitude, and Practices Related to Eye Health and Disease." Bethesda, MD: National Eye Institute and Lions Clubs International Foundation, 2007.

National Institute of Statistics of Rwanda. *Millennium Development Goals Country Report 2007*. Kigali: National Institute of Statistics of Rwanda, 2007.

Nishtar, S. "Public–Private 'Partnerships' in Health: A Global Call to Action." *Health Res Policy Syst* 2, no. 1 (2004): 5.

Novartis. "SMS for Life." Novartis, www.malaria.novartis.com/innovation/sms-for-life/index.shtml.

Novogratz, J. *The Blue Sweater: Bridging the Gap between Rich and Poor in an Interconnected World*. New York: Rodale, 2009.

Nussbaum, M.C. *Creating Capabilities: The Human Development Approach*. Cambridge, MA: Belknap Press of Harvard University Press, 2011.

Oxfam. "Education: Tackling the Global Crisis." Briefing Paper, Oxfam International, 2011.

Parham, G.P., et al. "Prevalence and Predictors of Squamous Intraepithelia Lesions of the Cervix in HIV-Infected Women in Lusaka, Zambia." *Gynecologic Oncology* 103, no. 3 (2006): 1017–22.

Parker, S. *The Life Cycle of Entrepreneurial Ventures*, vol. 3. New York: Springer, 2006.

Pastor, M., and R. Ortiz. "Making Change: How Social Movements Work and How to Support Them." In *Program for Environmental and Regional Equity*. Los Angeles: University of Southern California, 2009.

Patel, V., et al. "Effectiveness of an Intervention Led by Lay Health Counsellors for Depressive and Anxiety Disorders in Primary Care in Goa, India (Manas): A Cluster Randomised Control Trial." *Lancet* 376, no. 9758 (2010): 2086–95.

———. "Lay Health Worker–Led Intervention for Depressive and Anxiety Disorders in India: Impact on Clinical and Disability Outcomes over 12 Months." *British Journal of Psychiatry* 199, no. 6 (2011): 459–66.

PATH. *Annual Report 2011*. Seattle, WA: PATH, 2011.

Pfeiffer, J., et al. "Integration of HIV / AIDS Services into African Primary Health Care: Lessons Learned for Health System Strengthening in Mozambique: A Case Study." *J Int AIDS Soc* 13 (2010): 3.

Piette, J.D., et al. "Impacts of e-Health on the Outcomes of Care in Low- and Middle-Income Countries: Where Do We Go from Here?" *Bulletin of the World Health Organization* 90, no. 5 (2012): 365–72.

Pink Ribbon Red Ribbon. "About the Partnership." Pink Ribbon Red Ribbon, www.pinkandredribbon.com.

Piot, P. "Innovation and Technology for Global Public Health." *Global Public Health* 7, no. 1 (2012): 46–53.

Piot, P., and S. Ebrahim. "Prevention and Control of Chronic Diseases." *BMJ* 341 (2010).

Pisano, G.P. *The Development Factory: Unlocking the Potential of Process Innovation*. Boston: Harvard Business School Press, 1997.

Pop-Eleches, C., et al. "Mobile Phone Technologies Improve Adherence to Antiretroviral Treatment in a Resource-Limited Setting: A Randomized Controlled Trial of Text Message Reminders." *AIDS* 25, no. 6 (March 2011): 825–34.

Prahalad, C.K. *The Fortune at the Bottom of the Pyramid: Eradicating Poverty through Profits*. Upper Saddle River, NJ: Wharton School Publishing, 2010.

Prata, N., et al. "Training Traditional Birth Attendants to Use Misoprostol and an Absorbent Delivery Mat in Home Births." *Social Science & Medicine* 75, no. 11 (2012): 2021–28.

Prata, N., A. Gessessew, A. Cartwright, and A. Fraser. "Provision of Injectable Contraceptives in Ethiopia through Community-Based Reproductive Health Agents." *Bulletin of the World Health Organization* 89, no. 8 (2011): 556–64.

Prata, N., P. Passano, S. Bell, T. Rowen, and M. Potts. "New Hope: Community-Based Misoprostol Use to Prevent Postpartum Haemorrhage." *Health Policy and Planning* (August 2012).

Prata, N., A. Sreenivas, F. Vahidnia, and M. Potts. "Saving Maternal Lives in Resource-Poor Settings: Facing Reality." *Health Policy* 89, no. 2 (2009): 131–48.

Qiang, C.Z., M. Yamamichi, V. Hausman, R. Miller, and D. Altman. *Mobile Applications for the Health Sector.* Washington, DC: World Bank, 2012.

Qiao, Y., et al. "A New HPV-DNA Test for Cervical-Cancer Screening in Developing Regions: A Cross-Sectional Study of Clinical Accuracy in Rural China." *Lancet Oncology* 9, no. 10 (2008): 929–36.

Quint, J., H.S. Bloom, A.R. Black, and L. Stephens. "The Challenge of Scaling Up Educational Reform." New York: MDRC, 2005.

Quisumbing, A.R., L. Haddad, and C. Peña. "Are Women Overrepresented among the Poor? An Analysis of Poverty in 10 Developing Countries." *Journal of Development Economics* 66, no. 1 (2001): 225–69.

Radjou, N., J. Prabhu, and S. Ahuja. *Jugaad Innovation: Think Frugal, Be Flexible, Generate Breakthrough Growth.* San Francisco: Jossey-Bass, 2012.

Rahman, A., et al. "Cognitive Behaviour Therapy-Based Intervention by Community Health Workers for Mothers with Depression and Their Infants in Rural Pakistan: A Cluster-Randomised Controlled Trial." *Lancet* 372, no. 9642 (2008): 902–9.

Raju, N., et al. "Effect of Aspirin on Mortality in the Primary Prevention of Cardiovascular Disease." *American Journal of Medicine* 124, no. 7 (2011): 621–29.

Ramundo, K. "The Female 'Army' Leading Ethiopia's Health Revolution." *Frontlines*, May/June 2012.

Rannan-Eliya, R.P., ed. *Bangladesh National Health Accounts 1997–2007.* Data International Limited, 2010.

Ranson, M.K., et al. "Priorities for Research into Human Resources for Health in Low- and Middle-Income Countries." *Bulletin of the World Health Organization* 88, no. 6 (2010): 435–43.

Ravishankar, N., et al. "Financing of Global Health: Tracking Development Assistance for Health from 1990 to 2007." *Lancet* 373, no. 9681 (2009): 2113–24.

RDT Info. "Tests for Specific Diseases." PATH, www.rapid-diagnostics.org/tests.htm.

Riders for Health. "Our Approach." Riders for Health, http://www.riders.org/ what-we-do/our-approach.

Reich, M.R. "Public–Private Partnerships for Public Health." *Nature Medicine* 6, no. 6 (2000): 617–20.

Ritzer, G. *The McDonaldization of Society.* Thousand Oaks, CA: SAGE, 1993.

Roberts, L., et al. "Keeping Clean Water Clean in a Malawi Refugee Camp: A Randomized Intervention Trial." *Bulletin of the World Health Organization* 79, no. 4 (2001): 280–87.

Robinson, S. "Nkosi Johnson." *Time,* December 31, 2001.

Rothwell, P.M., et al. "Effect of Daily Aspirin on Risk of Cancer Metastasis: A Study of Incident Cancers during Randomised Controlled Trials." *Lancet* 279, no. 9826 (2012): 1591–601.

———. "Short-Term Effects of Daily Aspirin on Cancer Incidence, Mortality, and Non-Vascular Death: Analysis of the Time Course of Risks and Benefits in 51 Randomised Controlled Trials." *Lancet* 379, no. 9826 (2012): 1602–612.

Rutstein, S.O. "Effects of Preceding Birth Intervals on Neonatal, Infant and Under-Five Years Mortality and Nutritional Status in Developing Countries: Evidence from the Demographic and Health Surveys." *International Journal of Gynaecology and Obstetrics* 89, no. 1 (2005): 7.

Sachs, J. *The End of Poverty: Economic Possibilities for Our Time.* New York: Penguin Books, 2006.

Salter, C. "Narayana Hruduyalaya for Bringing Medical Care to the Masses." Fast Company, www.fastcompany.com/most-innovative-companies/2012/ narayana-hrudayalaya-hospitals.

Samoff, J., E.M. Sebatane, and M. Dembélé. "Scaling Up by Focusing Down: Creating Space to Expand Education Reform." Paper presented at the Biennial Meeting for the Association for the Development of Education in Africa, Arusha, Tanzania, 2001.

Sankaranarayanan, R., et al. "Effect of Visual Screening on Cervical Cancer Incidence and Mortality in Tamil Nadu, India: A Cluster-Randomised Trial." *Lancet* 370, no. 9585 (2007): 398–406.

Sedgh, G., S. Singh, I.H. Shah, E. Åhman, S.K. Henshaw, and A. Bankole. "Induced Abortion: Incidence and Trends Worldwide from 1995 to 2008." *Lancet* 379, no. 9816 (2012): 625–32.

Sehgal, V., K. Dehoff, and G. Panneer. "The Importance of Frugal Engineering." *Strategy+Business* (Summer 2010): 59.

Sellors, J., and R. Sankaranarayanan. "Treatment of Cervical Intraepithelial Neoplasia by Cryotherapy." Chapter 12 in *Colposcopy and Treatment of Cervical Intraepithelial Neoplasia: A Beginner's Manual.* Lyon, France: International Agency for Research on Cancer, 2003.

Sen, A. *Development as Freedom*. New York: Anchor, 2000.

Setty-Venugopal, V., and U. Upadhyay. "Birth Spacing: Three to Five Saves Lives." In *Population Reports*. Baltimore: Population Information Program, 2002.

Singh, S., and J.E. Darroch. "Adding It Up: Costs and Benefits of Contraceptive Services—Estimates for 2012." New York: Guttmacher Institute and UNFPA, 2012.

Singh, S., G. Sedgh, and R. Hussain. "Unintended Pregnancy: Worldwide Levels, Trends, and Outcomes." *Studies in Family Planning* 41, no. 4 (2010): 241–50.

Sireau, Nicolas. *Microfranchising: How Social Entrepreneurs Are Building a New Road to Development*. Sheffield, UK: Greenleaf, 2011.

Smillie, I. *Freedom from Want: The Remarkable Success Story of BRAC, the Global Grassroots Organization That's Winning the Fight against Poverty*. Sterling, VA: Kumarian Press, 2009.

Sobsey, M.D., et al. "Point of Use Household Drinking Water Filtration: A Practical, Effective Solution for Providing Sustained Access to Safe Drinking Water in the Developing World." *Environmental Science & Technology* 42, no. 12 (2008): 4261–67.

Spector, J.M., et al. "Improving Quality of Care for Maternal and Newborn Health: Prospective Pilot Study of the WHO Safe Childbirth Checklist Program." *PLOS ONE* 7, no. 5 (2012): e35151.

Stevenson, H. "Perspective on Entrepreneurship." *Harvard Business Review* (1983): 13.

———. "Why Entrepreneurship Has Won!" Harvard Business School, Coleman White Paper (2000).

Suares, L.R. *Real Money, New Frontiers*. Lancaster, UK: Gazelle, 2009.

Sudio, R.K., et al. "The Magnitude and Trend of Artemether-Lumefantrine Stock-outs at Public Health Facilities in Kenya." *Malaria Journal* 11 (2012): 37.

Sweat, M.D., J. Denison, C. Kennedy, V. Tedrow, and K. O'Reilly. "Effects of Condom Social Marketing on Condom Use in Developing Countries: A Systematic Review and Meta-analysis, 1990–2010." *Bulletin of the World Health Organization* 90, no. 8 (2012): 557–632.

Teklehaimanot, A,, J.D. Sachs, and C. Curtis. "Malaria Control Needs Mass Distribution of Insecticidal Bednets." *Lancet* 369, no. 9580 (2007): 2143–46.

Tomasini, R., and L.V. Wassenhove. *Humanitarian Logistics*. New York: Palgrave Macmillan, 2009.

Topp, S.M., et al. "Integrating HIV Treatment with Primary Care Outpatient Services: Opportunities and Challenges from a Scaled-up Model in Zambia." *Health Policy Plan* (2012).

———. "Strengthening Health Systems at Facility-Level: Feasibility of Integrating Antiretroviral Therapy into Primary Health Care Services in Lusaka,

Zambia." *PLOS ONE* 5, no. 7 (2010): e11522.

Torero, M., and S. Chowdhury. *Increasing Access to Infrastructure for Africa's Rural Poor.* Washington, DC: International Food Policy Research Institute, 2005.

Trussell J. "Contraceptive Efficacy." In Hatcher, R.A., et al. *Contraceptive Technology,* 20th rev ed. New York: Ardent Media, 2011.

Tushman, M., and P. Anderson. "Technological Discontinuities and Organizational Environment." *Administrative Science Quarterly* 31 (1986): 439–65.

Tushman, M., and J.P. Murmann. "Dominant Designs, Technology Cycles, and Organizational Outcomes." *Research in Organizational Behavior* 20 (1998): 231–66.

UNAIDS. "Global AIDS Response Continues to Show Results as a Record Number of People Access Treatment and Rates of New HIV Infections Fall by Nearly 25%." Geneva: UNAIDS, 2011.

———. *Global HIV/AIDS Response: Epidemic Update and Health Sector Progress towards Universal Access: Progress Report 2011.* Geneva: UNAIDS, 2011.

———. *Together We Will End Aids.* Geneva: UNAIDS, 2012.

———. *UNAIDS 2010 Global Report.* Geneva: UNAIDS, 2010.

UNDP. *Human Development Report 2011: Sustainability and Equality, A Better Future for All.* New York: UNDP, 2011.

———. *Towards Human Resilience: Sustaining MDG Progress in an Age of Economic Uncertainty.* New York: UNDP, 2011.

UNICEF. "Innovations: Uganda." Available at www.unicef.org/uganda/9903.html. Accessed October 30, 2012.

———. *Facts for Life, Fourth Edition.* New York: UNICEF, 2010.

———. *Levels & Trends in Child Mortality.* New York: UNICEF, 2010.

———. *The State of the World's Children 2007.* New York: UNICEF, 2007.

———. *The State of the World's Children 2012.* New York: UNICEF, 2012.

United Nations Industrial Development Organization. *Creating an Enabling Environment for Private Sector Development in Sub-Saharan Africa.* Vienna: United Nations Industrial Development Organization (UNIDO), 2008.

United Nations Maternal Health Task Force and Global Health Visions. *UN Commission on Life Saving Commodities for Women and Children: Country Case Studies.* New York: UN Commission on Life-Saving Commodities for Women and Children, 2012.

United Nations Population Fund. "Maternal Mortality Reduction Programme in Rwanda." Kigali, Rwanda: UNFPA Rwanda Office.

USAID. *A Vision for Health: Performance-Based Financing in Rwanda.* Washington, DC: USAID, 2009.

Utterback, J.M. *Mastering the Dynamics of Innovation: How Companies Can Seize Opportunities in the Face of Technological Change.* Boston: Harvard Business School Press, 1994.

Verpoorten, M. "The Death Toll of the Rwandan Genocide: A Detailed Analysis for Gikongoro Province." *Population* 60, no. 4 (2005): 331–67.

Vickers, T. "Driving Down the Cost of High-Quality Care: Lessons from the Aravind Eye Care System." *Health International*, 2011.

VisionSpring. "Partners: BRAC." VisionSpring, www.visionspring.org/what-we-do/partners-detail.php?id=6.

———. "VisionSpring at a Glance." VisionSpring, www.visionspring.org/about/at-a-glance.php.

———. "What We Do: The Vision Entrepreneur." VisionSpring, http://www.visionspring.org/what-we-do/ve.php.

Wakabi, W. "Extension Workers Drive Ethiopia's Primary Health Care." *Lancet* 372, no. 9642 (2008): 880.

Wang et al. (2012) "Age-Specific and Sex-Specific Mortality in 187 Countries, 1970–2010: A Systematic Analysis for the Global Burden of Disease Study 2010."

W.K. Kellogg Foundation. *Logic Model Development Guide.* Battle Creek, MI: W.K. Kellogg Foundation, 2004.

World Alliance for Patient Safety. "Implementation Manual Surgical Safety Checklist: Safe Surgery Saves Lives." Geneva: WHO, 2008, www.who.int/patientsafety/safesurgery/en/index.html.

———. *Africa Development Indicators.* Washington, DC: World Bank, 2006.

World Health Organization. "Cardiovascular Diseases (CVDs) Fact Sheet." Geneva: WHO, www.who.int/mediacentre/factsheets/fs348/en/index.html.

———. "Children: Reducing Mortality Fact Sheet." Geneva: WHO, www.who.int/mediacentre/factsheets/fs178/en/index.html.

———. *Classifying Health Workers: Mapping Occupations to the International Standard Classification.* Geneva: WHO, 2012.

———. "Depression Fact Sheet." Geneva: WHO, http://www.who.int/mediacentre/factsheets/fs369/en/index.html.

———. "Diarrhoeal Disease Fact Sheet." Geneva: WHO, www.who.int/mediacentre/factsheets/fs330/en/index.html.

———. "Family Planning Fact Sheet." Geneva: WHO, www.who.int/mediacentre/factsheets/fs351/en/index.html.

———. *The Global Burden of Disease: 2004 Update.* Geneva: WHO, 2008.

———. *Global Data on Visual Impairments, 2010.* Geneva: WHO, 2012.

———. *Global HIV/AIDS Response Progress Report 2011.* Geneva: WHO, 2011.

———. "HIV/AIDS Fact Sheet." Geneva: WHO, www.who.int/mediacentre/factsheets/fs360/en/index.html.

———. *Investing in Maternal, Newborn, and Child Health: The Case for Asia and the Pacific.* Geneva: WHO, 2009.

————. *Maternal Health: Investing in the Lifeline of Healthy Societies and Economies.* Geneva: WHO, 2010.

————. "Maternal Mortality Fact Sheet." Geneva: WHO, www.who.int/mediacentre/factsheets/fs348/en/index.html.

————. *mHealth: New Horizons for Health Through Mobile Technologies.* Geneva: WHO, 2011.

————. *Monitoring Emergency Obstetric Care: A Handbook.* Geneva: WHO, 2009.

————. "More Research Needed Into Childhood Diarrhoea." Geneva: WHO, 2009.

————. *Oral Rehydration Salts: Production of the New ORS.* Geneva:WHO, 2006.

————. "Pneumonia Fact Sheet." Geneva: WHO, www.who.int/mediacentre/factsheets/fs331/en/index.html.

————. *Prevention of Cardiovascular Disease: Guidelines for Assessment and Management of Cardiovascular Risk.* Geneva: WHO, 2007.

————. *Prevention of Cervical Cancer through Screening Using Visual Inspection with Acetic Acid (VIA) and Treatment with Cryotherapy: A Demonstration Project in Six African Countries: Malawi, Madagascar, Nigeria, Uganda, the United Republic of Tanzania, and Zambia.* Geneva: WHO, 2012.

————. *Stop the Global Epidemic of Chronic Disease: A Practical Guide to Successful Advocacy.* Ed. by J. Epping-Jordan. Geneva: WHO, 2006.

————. "The Top 10 Causes of Death." Geneva: WHO, www.who.int/mediacentre/factsheets/fs310/en/index.html.

————. *Trends in Maternal Mortality 1990 to 2010.* Geneva: WHO, 2012.

————. "Visual Impairment and Blindness Fact Sheet." Geneva: WHO, www.who.int/mediacentre/factsheets/fs282/en/index.html.

————. "Voluntary Medical Male Circumcision for HIV Prevention Fact Sheet." Geneva: WHO, www.who.int/hiv/topics/malecircumcision/fact_sheet/en/index.html.

————. *World Health Report 2005.* Geneva: WHO, 2005.

————. *World Health Statistics 2011.* Geneva: WHO, 2011.

————. *World Health Statistics 2012.* Geneva: WHO, 2012.

————. *World Malaria Report 2010.* Geneva: WHO, 2010.

————. *World Malaria Report 2011.* Geneva: WHO, 2011.

————. *World Malaria Report 2012.* Geneva: WHO, 2012.

WHO and UNICEF. *Countdown to 2015: Maternal, Newborn, and Child Survival.* Geneva: WHO and UNICEF, 2010.

WHO, UNICEF, and UNFPA. *Maternal Mortality 2000.* Geneva: WHO, 2000.

WHO, UNICEF, and World Bank. *State of the World's Vaccines and Immunization,* 3rd ed. Geneva: WHO, 2009.

William J. Clinton Foundation. "News: Making Malaria Medications More Affordable," available at http://clintonfoundation.org/news/news-media/ making-malaria-medications-more-affordable. Accessed April 20, 2011.

Williams, M. "Rice's Student-Designed Device to Help Babies Breathe Wins More Support." *Rice University News & Media*, July 27, 2012.

Wilson, A., et al. "Effectiveness of Strategies Incorporating Training and Support of Traditional Birth Attendants on Perinatal and Maternal Mortality: Meta-Analysis." *BMJ: British Medical Journal* 343 (2011).

World Bank. *Private Sector Assessment for Health, Nutrition and Population (HNP) in Bangladesh*. Washington, DC: World Bank, 2004.

World Bicycle Relief. "Impact." Chicago: World Bicycle Relief, http://worldbicyclerelief.org/pages/impact.

———. *Impact of Bicycle Distribution on Tsunami Recovery in Sri Lanka, Final Report*. Chicago: World Bicycle Relief, 2007.

Yoong, J., et al., "Private Sector Participation and Health System Performance in Sub-Saharan Africa." *PLOS ONE* 5 (2010): e13243.

You, D., R. New, and T. Wardlaw. *Levels & Trends in Child Mortality: Report 2012*. New, York: UNICEF, 2012.

Yunas, M., and K. Weber. *Building Social Business: The New Kind of Capitalism That Serves Humanity's Most Pressing Needs*. New York: Public Affairs, 2010.

———. *Creating a World Without Poverty: Social Business and the Future of Capitalism*. New York: Public Affairs, 2007.

Zafar Ullah, A.N., et al. "Government–NGO Collaboration: The Case of Tuberculosis in Bangladesh." *Health Policy and Planning* 21, no. 2 (2006): 143–55.

Zambrano, R., and R.K. Seward. *Mobile Technologies and Empowerment: Enhancing Human Development through Participation and Innovation*. New York: United Nations Development Programme, 2012.

Zuckerman, E. "Web 2.0 Tools for Development: Simple Tools for Smart People." *Participatory Learning and Action* 59, no. 1 (2009): 87–94.

Index

A

accountability
  establishing goals and monitoring,
    3, 15, 21, 28, 42, 73–74, 83, 106,
    152, 157, 158–62, 170
  monitoring *versus* evaluation, 162
  and patient flows, 137
African Infectious Disease Villages
  Clinics (AIDVC), 60
AMUA (Marie Stopes), 114
Animateurs de Santé, 106
antiretroviral drugs, 14, 126, 126–27
Aravind Eye Center, 66, 168
  maximizing efficiency by, 20,
    139–41, 144
Ascension Health, 138

B

BabyCenter, 115
Bangladesh, 39, 111, 113, 115, 141,
  143
  birth attendants in, 73
  franchises in, 39, 66, 113
  health care challenges, 153
  program scaling in, 86
  voucher use in, 73
Becton Dickinson, 124
Bhagwan Mahaveer Viklang
  Sahayata Samiti, 40
Bicycle Empowerment Namibia, 60

bikes and motorcycles
  use in task shifting, 59–60
Bill and Melinda Gates Foundation,
  101, 125, 168
birth attendants and midwives,
  49, 55, 70–71, 73, 82, 99, 102, 103,
  108–10, 112
  as entrepreneurs, 71
birth control pills, 98
blood testing, 30
Blue Star, 39
Blue Star Bangladesh, 66
BlueStar network (Marie Stopes),
  113, 114
BRAC, 85, 153
  partnership with VisionSpring,
    142–43
  Social Innovation Lab, 153–54
Brazil, 107, 109, 126, 186
breastfeeding, 61, 62, 68, 99, 102,
  103, 115
Bristol Myers Squibb Foundation,
  124
Burundi, 168
Bush, Barbara P., 168
Bush, George W., 15, 128
  commitment to fighting AIDS,
    14, 124
business model innovation, 30–31,
  32

About the Authors

Eric G. Bing, MD, PhD, MBA, is Senior Fellow and Director of Global Health at the George W. Bush Institute and Professor of Global Health at Southern Methodist University in Dallas, Texas. He received his medical degree from Harvard Medical School, his PhD in Epidemiology from UCLA, and his MBA from the Fuqua School of Business at Duke University. Dr. Bing combines his training in  medicine and business to help solve global health challenges. He has taught health care management, consulted for health ministries, and developed and directed NGOs in Africa, Latin America, and the United States.

As the Director of Global Health at the George W. Bush Institute he partners with others to turn innovative ideas into practical health care solutions that can be tested, implemented, and scaled.

Marc J. Epstein, MBA, PhD, is Distinguished Research Professor of Management at Jones Graduate School of Business at Rice University in Houston, Texas. Prior to joining Rice, Dr. Epstein was a professor at Stanford Business School, Harvard Business School, and INSEAD (European Institute of Business Administration). In both academic research and managerial practice, Dr. Epstein is considered one of the global luminaries in the areas of sustainability, governance, performance measurement, and accountability in both corporations and nonprofit organizations. His 20 authored or co-authored books and over 100 professional articles include many award winners, including *Making Innovation Work: How to Manage It, Measure It, and Profit from It* (2006) and *Making Sustainability Work: Best Practices in Managing and Measuring Corporate Social, Environmental, and Economic Impacts* (2008).

Dr. Epstein is also currently working extensively in developing countries in Africa, Asia, and South America on microfinance, entrepreneurship, education, and the commercialization and dissemination of low-cost health technologies. In the middle of his MBA class, all of his students travel with him to Rwanda or Liberia to work on the commercialization of health technologies for the poor.

George W. Bush
Institute
★ ★ ★

The George W. Bush Institute is the policy research arm of the George W. Bush Presidential Center in Dallas, Texas. Founded by George and Laura Bush in 2009, the Bush Institute has the mission of advancing freedom by expanding opportunities for individuals at home and across the globe. Built on principles that guided the Bushes in public life, the Bush Institute uses leading research to develop and implement policies that offer practical solutions to pressing problems in the United States and abroad. The Bush Institute has four policy areas focused on Education Reform, Human Freedom, Global Health, and Economic Growth. Across all of its programs, the Institute integrates women and veterans through the Women's Initiative and Military Service Initiative.

Part of the mission of the Bush Institute is to promote sustainable global health solutions in developing countries, with a focus on the continent of Africa. The Bush Institute creates measurable improvements in health through an emphasis on data-driven decisions and local control, accountability and responsibility. The Institute concentrates on cost-effective disease prevention and treatment services that address health conditions throughout a person's life.

Berrett–Koehler
Publishers

A community dedicated to creating
a world that works for all

Visit Our Website: www.bkconnection.com

Read book excerpts, see author videos and Internet movies, read our authors' blogs, join discussion groups, download book apps, find out about the BK Affiliate Network, browse subject-area libraries of books, get special discounts, and more!

Subscribe to Our Free E-Newsletter, the *BK Communiqué*

Be the first to hear about new publications, special discount offers, exclusive articles, news about bestsellers, and more! Get on the list for our free e-newsletter by going to **www.bkconnection.com**.

Get Quantity Discounts

Berrett-Koehler books are available at quantity discounts for orders of ten or more copies. Please call us toll-free at (800) 929-2929 or email us at bkp .orders@aidcvt.com.

Join the BK Community

BKcommunity.com is a virtual meeting place where people from around the world can engage with kindred spirits to create a world that works for all. BKcommunity.com members may create their own profiles, blog, start and participate in forums and discussion groups, post photos and videos, answer surveys, announce and register for upcoming events, and chat with others online in real time. Please join the conversation!